STOPPING

STOPPING

*How to Be Still When
You Have to Keep Going*

Dr. David Kundtz

Foreword by Richard Carlson

MJF Books
NEW YORK

All acknowledgements of permission to reprint previously published material can be found on pp. 269-70, which constitute an extension of this copyright page.

Published by MJF Books
Fine Communications
Two Lincoln Square
60 West 66th Street
New York, NY 10023

Stopping
Library of Congress Catalog Card Number 98-67584
ISBN 1-56731-292-6

Copyright © 1998 by David Kundtz, S.T.D.

This edition published by arrangement with Conari Press.
Cover Painting: "Pears on Windowsill" by Marnie Johnson
Cover Design: Ame Beanland
Book Design and Composition: Jennifer Brontsema
Chart on Page 135: John Lomibao Design

Manufactured in the United States of America on acid-free paper

MJF Books and the MJF colophon are trademarks of Fine Creative Media, Inc.

10   9   8   7   6   5   4   3   2   1

*To the memory of my father
whose example taught me about Stopping.
To the memory of my mother
who always encouraged me to write.*

CONTENTS

Foreword

When I first looked at *Stopping: How to Be Still When You Have to Keep Going*, I realized immediately that I was in familiar territory. In fact, it didn't take me long to locate in my own work a very specific expression of what *Stopping* is all about: "Virtually every day, I stop whatever I'm doing to enjoy the sunrise. . ." *(Don't Sweat the Small Stuff. . . and it's all small stuff)*. And this is just one of many examples. Yes, Stopping as defined by Dr. Kundtz—doing nothing in order to wake up and remember who you are—is something that has been part of my life for a long time.

What we owe David Kundtz is credit for conceptualizing a simple yet profound reality and offering to us an elegant and powerful tool for finding the serenity and stillness that so easily escapes us as we cope with too-busy lives.

Stopping is a happy marriage of the riches of many of the world's contemplative and mystical traditions, with the insight and awareness of contemporary psychology. Just what the world needs right now, it seems to me.

Finally, because it gives us perspective, because it encourages us to put first things first, and because it keeps us awake and aware, Stopping is an ideal way to remember something important about the vast majority of things that bother and upset us: It's all small stuff.

—Richard Carlson, Ph.D.

I

Stopping
at the
Speed of Light

*The dogmas of the quiet past, are inadequate
to the stormy present. . . .
As our case is new, so we must think anew
and act anew.*

ABRAHAM LINCOLN

1

Facing the Mountain of Too Much

"It's too much," Mary Helen told me, "way too much. I
just can't deal with it all!" Then she gave in to tears. Mary
Helen, a successful and intelligent woman of thirty-eight,
with a thriving career and a loving family, was close to the
end of her rope.

Any observer in my counseling office that day would
clearly have seen that Mary Helen was in trouble: anxious,
stressed, unfocused, irritable, unable to sleep, overwhelmed by life, and frustrated with her inability to manage it. She was angry at herself for her inability to cope
and angry at me because I was the one to whom she had
admitted it.

Although she was not aware of it, she did know what the problem was. It was the first thing she said: "too much." Upon further exploration, I found no underlying psychosis, no debilitating personality disorder, no family-of-origin dysfunction making a sudden midlife appearance, nor a marriage about to crash on the rocks of incompatibility. Just that life had become too much.

Just that life had become too much? Hardly. Although the problem may seem well known, its vastness, depth, and long-term implications are still far from our conscious recognition. As with any hidden enemy, the contemporary problem of too much has its way with all of us. The damage is extremely severe and is sometimes even life threatening.

Do you sometimes feel like Mary Helen, overwhelmed or emotionally numbed by the pace and sheer quantity of life? Are you reluctantly prevented by your overloaded schedule from keeping your true priorities? Do you feel unable to do all the things you need to do and still have time for yourself? Have you come to realize that it's been too long since you've enjoyed real, satisfying, and regular leisure? If so, you've found the right book.

Do you have a desire to give more attention to the spiritual aspects of your life—your truly important meanings and values—but have been frustrated in trying to transform that desire into a real practice? You will find nourishment here.

Or have you been frustrated with complicated, time-consuming, or impractical systems of meditation and slowing down that don't really work for you? You can anticipate success through the suggestions found in this book.

Most of us in this hurry-up, e-mail world of instant response are feeling the same sense of overload that my client Mary Helen felt. Indeed, the primary challenge to successful human life in the postmodern, millennial world is the challenge of too much: too much to do; too much to cope with; too much distraction; too much noise; too much demanding our attention; or, for many of us, too many opportunities and too many choices. Too much of everything for the time and energy available.

We all have been feeling, at least on a subliminal level, the choices, demands, and complexities of life increase with every passing year. We have more to be, more to do, more places to go, and more things we want or need to accomplish. But the day remains twenty-four hours; the year, the same twelve months. The amount of activity constantly increases, but both the amount of time into which it must fit and the human energy with which it must be met, at best, remain the same.

Even though my client Mary Helen named her problem—"It's way too much. I just can't deal with it all"—she didn't recognize it, first, as something very serious and, second, as something new. Rather, she saw it just as one more of life's irritations that she should be able to deal with. This attitude reveals a key characteristic of the problem of too much: It passes itself off as something it is not. It says, "I am the same old problem you have been dealing with all your life, you can handle me." But the reality is that we can't—and believing we can is part and parcel of the problem.

Why don't we see it coming? The answer is as simple as it is clear: it is masquerading, and the purpose of a masquerade is to make you think it's something else. We are all like Mary Helen, saying to ourselves, "This should not be a serious problem!" Because it looks and feels like the same old problem of being just too busy and in the past we have been able to handle it with the coping strategies available to us, we miss its seriousness and power.

It's time to rip off the mask from the problem of too much and reveal the seriously damaging monster that is destroying too many lives and too many families. Modern life has become impossible to cope with in the same old ways we learned as children and young adults.

That's because the sheer amount of too much also makes it a new and essentially different challenge. Consider this for a moment, because at first it might not seem evident: Precisely because of the very large volume of the same old thing, it has become essentially different. It is not just a larger amount of the same thing, but is something entirely new.

It's like the evolution of a pile of rocks into a mountain.

At some point in its history it stops being a pile of rocks and starts being a mountain. When exactly does that happen? The transition point would be difficult to determine. Does this last eruption finally make it a mountain or must we wait for one more? So it is with the problem of too much: it has become what it is over a long period of time. For most of us, the point at which too much has become a mountain is long past. What used to be a pile of rocks has become the Mountain of Too Much.

It is vital to recognize this mountain as new because it is the newness that signifies the need for different coping strategies to conquer it. The tools needed to conquer a pile of rocks are very different from those demanded by a mountain. So it is as we face the Mountain of Too Much. A sturdy pair of shoes is sufficient for a pile of rocks, but an imposing peak demands carabiners, belaying systems, and training in specific skills.

Mary Helen, my bright, normally fun-loving and competent client, was truly puzzled. "Why can't I deal with this? I have always been able to cope, even when things have been difficult. Why not now?" But this was a new and challenging mountain, not just the same old pile of rocks she had walked over many times before. But *that* was what she needed to see.

So it is with all of us—we keep dealing with the problem of too much in the same old ways we learned before the pile of rocks became a mountain. As a result, we are overstressed, overloaded, overtired, and unable to solve the serious problems and challenges that are a direct result of our revved-up pace of life. It's time to learn a different way to face our Mountain of Too Much and to trade in our old ways of coping for new ones.

No matter how fast we go,
no matter how many comforts we forgo . . .
there never seems to be enough time.

JAY WALLJASPER

2

Why Cramming and Cutting Don't Work

In the past, we used two ways of coping with the challenge of too much: We crammed things in or we cut things out. These are natural, normal, and effective responses to life at a certain pace.

Cramming is trying to fit more and more into the same, limited time and space using the same, limited energy and stamina. Until the pile of rocks changed into the Mountain of Too Much, cramming worked just fine: We became more efficient and more productive. We learned to manage our time better, to move faster, and to sprint through our day without pausing for breath. But that was before we reached the critical mass of too much. Now it causes us to be overwhelmed and stuffed to overfull; thus, we are left frustrated and feeling like we have no room left for ourselves. Whenever I feel this stuffed feeling, I often show it through moodiness, irritability, and spiritual malaise.

Think of packing your suitcase. Have you ever tried to cram things in? You cram and cram and even resort to sitting on it to force it closed, but there is a moment when, with just one more pair of socks, the suitcase will not close. And even if we manage to jam the suitcase shut, we may rip its seams or risk it popping open in mid-flight. Think of yourself as that suitcase: Your seams are ripping and your emotional insides are bursting out and spilling into the middle of your day. That's the point we're at. Cramming no longer works. There is simply too much to fit in.

Cutting out is excluding things from our lives to make more room for new demands. We become good at prioritizing: We drop old friends to make room for taking our kids to soccer, we eliminate lunch to get a little more work done, we cut short our days off to catch up on a report, and we wake up an hour early to have time for exercise. But this works only to a certain point. Finally, you can cut out no more. You get down to the essentials: work, personal responsibilities, and a necessary amount of sleep and social time. When demands from work or family crises intervene, leisure time, exercise, social life, and days off go out the window. Finally, there comes a time when there is nothing to cut and still too much to do. Our health—mental and physical—suffers. We voice the complaint that I hear most often in my seminars on stress: We feel as though we are moving through life, but not actually *experiencing* it. As you probably know from your own life, cutting just no longer works.

The Mountain of Too Much is new and therefore calls for new skills. It's long past the time to let go of these once-effective responses. They are ineffective habits of behavior. They are also a form of denial, that which is a lack of awareness of a situation too painful or disturbing to acknowledge in this case the problem of too much. Besides being futile, these habits are robbing us of the pleasure of life.

But there is something new that you can learn to do. I call it Stopping.

3

Doing Nothing

The first time I became aware of Stopping, I was hiding. I was on the run and felt lost. I was trying to figure out what to do with my life and didn't really know what was happening to me or how it would all turn out.

I had been a successful and content Catholic priest for fifteen years, but all of a sudden I was in crisis. Nothing felt right anymore. My enthusiasm for my vocation had abandoned me. For the first time in my life I felt lonely. I avoided responsibilities, denied what was happening, and made some foolish decisions. Finally, not knowing what to do, I stopped doing everything. I escaped to a small, isolated cabin, perched high on a hill overlooking the Pacific Ocean on the northern California coast, for a month to figure it out.

I just stopped. And in so doing, I found my way again. I didn't stop on purpose, but it was the best thing I could have done for myself. It was not until much later, after many occasions of Stopping, some as short as ten seconds and others as long as a month, that I became conscious of its value and could actually define it:

Stopping is doing nothing as much as possible, for a definite period of time (one second to one month) for the purpose of becoming more fully awake and remembering who you are.

This is the simple practice upon which this book is built, a new skill to replace cramming and cutting that can help deal with the Mountain of Too Much. Doing nothing should not be confused with a total lack of activity. Doing nothing is indeed doing something very important. It's allowing life to happen—your life. Doing nothing is something quite profound.

The ultimate purpose of Stopping is to ensure that when we do go, we go in the direction that we want and that we are not just reacting to the pace of our lives, but choosing, moment by moment, what's best. The ultimate reason for Stopping is going. Going is what we of the industrialized Western world are known for. It's what we do best: get on with business, get things done, accomplish feats, and assume roles of leadership and power. So Stopping at first glance might not seem so desirable, it may even appear to be opposed to our fundamental values. But, not only is it *not* against these values, Stopping maintains and cultivates them. Without being awake and remembering our values and identity—in other words, without Stopping—our going can get us into deep trouble.

Stopping, even in its shortest form, allows you to realize the essential meanings of your life and to consistently remember what is truly important to you so you can keep your priorities in order and up-to-date. It helps you know what you want to achieve and how you want to behave.

Stopping works where cramming and cutting don't, because it calls a time-out and gives you the freedom to reorganize the game of life according to your own rules; to recognize your true priorities. It creates an oasis where the turbulent waters caused by the demands of daily life can quiet and where, in the stillness, you can again see your own reflection. It gives you time to *be*, not just to *do*.

Stopping is born of personal experience and, like many useful ideas, came to me because I needed it so badly. In most cases, we don't stop until we feel overwhelmed and don't know where to turn. For some reason, when I got to the end of my rope, I just did nothing and waited, not out of any virtuous inclination, not because I thought the waiting would solve anything, but because I didn't know what else to do.

Now I can look back and see the value in that time of waiting: There were moments, short and long (but mostly short), in which I remembered some important information about myself, became more awake to my life, and became aware of all the aspects involved in the issue I was dealing with. Stopping helped me get going again, but going in a focused and determined way, rather than a scattered and chaotic one.

So this book is about Stopping, and specifically about Stopping when you feel you have to keep going. This kind of quieting and self-remembering is designed specifically to fit the needs of people who must live their lives at an ever-increasing speed and with an overwhelming number of demands upon them. And because that description fits many of us, chances are *you* are feeling overwhelmed and overloaded in your life and are looking for something—anything—to relieve the strain. If so, you've come to the right place. Stopping will help. And it's easy. You can do it anywhere at anytime.

The fast-paced rhythm of modern life conditions
us to skim the surface of experience,
then quickly move on to something new.

STEPHAN RECHTSCHAFFEN

4

A Fast Train on the Fast Track

Stopping is not slowing down. There are many books on slowing down the frantic pace of life. This is not one of them, even though an important aspect of Stopping—even one of the reasons for Stopping—is, in fact, to slow down. The process of Stopping is very different from the process of slowing down. Trying to slow down does not slow you down. We have been trying to do that for many years now; it generally doesn't work. It's like trying to cut down on smoking: in a short time you end up where you started, except more frustrated.

Slowing down doesn't work because everything around us is going so fast. We get revved-up even if we don't want to be. In his book *Timeshifting*, Stephan

Rechtschaffen, M.D., writes about *entrainment*, which he describes as an unconscious "process that governs how various rhythms fall into sync with one another." For example, if you were to place two out-of-sync pendulum clocks next to one another, in a short time they would be exactly in sync. "The same principle works," says Rechtschaffen, "with atomic particles, the tides and human beings." With human beings? That's quite a remarkable idea. We pick up each other's rhythms and the accumulated rhythms of the world around us. If most of the rhythms around us are fast, so are ours, automatically. That's entrainment. The word can also mean "getting on a train."

We have all boarded the train, the fast train on the fast track, and the process of entrainment is not under our conscious control. That's why *trying* to slow down doesn't slow us down. It's not because we're weak willed or quitters; it's because we're on a fast train where we're the passengers and not the engineers.

We are all riding on a very fast train that is traveling down a predetermined track, gathering speed as it goes, and we have been on it for a long time. We can't get to the engineer because the engineer is protected by loyal guards. Or perhaps there really is no engineer; the train is run by a computer. Many of us want to slow down; some want to get off the train. Others are so used to the speed that they don't notice it. A few love the speed and want to increase it. The few who love the speed are the only ones who get their way. Most of us stare blankly out the window, barely seeing the world flying by and feeling helpless.

Fortunately, there is something we can do about it. Stopping can get us off the train, can separate us from the speeded-up rhythms of those around us, and can bring us into rhythms of our own choosing, which, it's important to note, may well include *some* time on the fast train. Stopping can roll us into the roundhouse for refreshment and cooling off so we can make sure that, when we take off again, we're on the right track, going in the right direction, and have a very intimate working relationship with the engineer.

Entrainment helps to explain the amazingly short attention span of most of us these days. We get our information in sound bites: many brief, skeletal bones of facts. We just don't have time to read in depth or to linger over the newspaper. It seems also to have something to say about our fad-driven society. As soon as one idea, trend, fashion, or person becomes popular, it is quickly dropped for whatever next demands our attention. Whether it is valuable or vulgar seems to make no difference; it's just the next view out the window of the fast train. Fad-driven culture engenders frenetic citizens who find themselves, unwittingly, screaming through the night on the fast train and trying to figure out, "How did I get here?"

Stopping can bring us both an answer and a solution.

It's good to have an end to journey toward;
but it's the journey that matters, in the end.

URSULA K. LEGUIN

5

Stopping at the Speed of Light

Stopping is paradoxical. It would at first seem, would
it not, that if one just stops, that is, does nothing, that it
would be a waste of time? Indeed, a way to describe doing
nothing is "wasting time." And when you feel stressed
and have too much to do, doing nothing may feel like the
worst approach. But paradoxically, doing nothing turns
out to be not only *not* a waste of time, but some of the
most significant time you can spend, even if it is only for
one minute.

This idea flies in the face of current belief and practice;
"Do more and do it more quickly" is what we hear. But it
is exactly this attitude that has made us overwhelmed.
What we've been doing isn't working.

The kind of Stopping that I am suggesting is done while moving *at the speed of light*. Stopping while moving at the speed of light is a paradox: To stop on the one hand and to go at the speed of light on the other are contradictory statements that create so radical a paradox that they appear to be an oxymoron. In other words, it doesn't make sense—unless you see it paradoxically! Then it is transformed into an exquisite, inviting, alluring, and richly textured truth: Time spent doing nothing allows us to awaken what is most meaningful and valuable to us.

This soulful truth is actually based on a scientific paradox. The amazing fact is that objects moving at the speed of light no longer experience time. In other words, at the speed of light, time stands still. Scientists assure me that these are true and accurate statements. I don't pretend to understand them scientifically, but I like them. And I like to apply them to Stopping: Stopping is time standing still or standing still in time.

Stopping at the speed of light acknowledges that the Stopping takes place within the context of a very fast world that waits for no one and, if you can't keep up, will leave you behind. It also acknowledges something that many people who teach spirituality are resistant to accept: going fast is not necessarily bad. Many of the "technologies that promote speed are essentially good. The historical record is that human beings have never, ever opted for slowness," says Jay Walljasper, an editor at *The Utne Reader*. "When I hear friends complain that their lives move too fast, they're not talking about a wholesale rejection of speed so much as a wish that they could spend more of their time involved in slow, contemplative activities." The problem, of course, is that there is way too much of one and not enough of the other. Stopping can restore the balance.

Many of us love the "revved-up beat of dance music, the fast-breaking action of basketball, or the speedy thrill of a roller coaster, but we don't want to live all our lives at that pace," says Walljasper. "A balanced life with intervals of creative frenzy giving way to relaxed tranquillity—is what people crave." Yes—and that's what Stopping is about.

The ultimate purpose of Stopping is going. But Stopping at the speed of light is not an unfulfilling, endless switching back and forth between going too fast and being dead still. Rather it brings its results—its gifts—to the person, not to the rate of speed. Its wonders are worked in the soul and thus are part of the person no matter what the speed of the moment.

Stopping ten times in a very hectic, emotionally demanding day doesn't feel like a jerky motion, but feels like a smooth flow moving in a balanced way through the day. The results are that you come to the end of the day not limp, exhausted, and depressed, but okay and, with appropriate rest, ready to continue with enthusiasm.

If families just let the culture happen to them,
they end up fat, addicted, broke,
with a house full of junk and no time.

MARY PIPHER

6

Intentional Living:
from Routine to Choice

It used to be that people didn't need Stopping *per se* because the natural rhythms of life provided sufficient time for them to achieve a sense of balance between quiet work and active work. There were busy times and leisure times and they tended to balance one another. It was just the way life was.

This balance was probably the common experience of our grandparents or great-grandparents. The pace of life allowed for time in between events: the time walking to school, to a neighbor's, or to church; and the time of solitary work around the house, shop, or farm. Life on the land was hard, but there were long stretches of winter

when people were homebound and the pace slowed to
a crawl.

I can remember, as a boy, loving to drive out with my
grandfather to his pig farm in rural northern Ohio. This
was in the late '40s. To me, my grandfather was bigger
than life. He was serious but kindly, had an Irish twinkle in
his eye, and always greeted me with,"Davit me bye!" My
mother was reluctant to let me go with him because I
would invariably come home a mess and late for dinner.
My grandfather would spend hours checking on the pigs
and talking to the farmer who ran the place. But what I
did was truly magical. I wandered around the farm—probably never out of eyeshot, or at least earshot, of my grandfather—and explored everything: the barn; the old, rusted
machinery; the pigs (I never got too close); and the fields. I
was doing nothing but fussin' around, poking about, loafing, hangin' out, and kickin' back.

For most of us (isn't it sad to think of kids deprived of
these aimless times?) such moments don't happen very
often any more. They aren't built into the pace of life; we're
just too busy. Picture these scenes in your mind's eye:

*On a leafy street in a small town, suburb, or residential part of
the city, a woman in her fifties, with graying hair, a calm look on
her face, and wearing a simple house dress and apron, is seated in
a rocking chair on her front porch on a warm summer afternoon.
Her kids are somewhere in the house, in the yard, or off doing
things. Her husband is working on the car in the back. From time
to time she hears the laughter and shouts of the neighbors' kids*

playing in a yard nearby. She is shelling fresh peas for dinner. The work is so familiar that she does it methodically, automatically, and without having to think about it. She takes the peas from the colander, separates peas from pods with a practiced movement of her hand, and drums the fresh peas into a bowl. She rocks slowly. Some moments she thinks of the things that need to be done in her yard: The grass needs cutting, I'll have to remind Tommy *and* Those nasturtiums are taking over everything, I think I'll pull them up and plant some geraniums. *Then she's a million miles away, remembering an event from her own childhood;* My how I loved to do that, *she says to no one and to anyone. The mailman interrupts this reverie and she chats with him a few moments, catching up with his rounds, his arthritis, and the neighbors' comings and goings. The mailman leaves and she sees that among the four pieces of mail is a letter from her sister in Denver. She puts that letter on top and places the little stack of mail on the porch railing. She glances at the letter and looks forward to opening it. She wonders if it has some news about their brother's health and, as she thinks of him, she offers a quick prayer. When she finishes her work and washes her hands, she'll enjoy taking a few moments to read the letter. This whole scene takes maybe twenty minutes or a half hour.*

The banker is writing at his desk. His pen runs dry. He carefully blots the work that he has been doing and puts it aside. He reaches for his inkwell, unscrews the barrel of his pen, and dips it carefully into the inkwell. He engages the lever that will draw ink into the reservoir and pauses to allow the excess ink to spill back into the well. He then reaches into his drawer for a specially kept, small, soft, ink-stained piece of cloth and uses it to wipe the ink from the surface of his pen. He folds and replaces the cloth in the

drawer, puts the two parts of the pen together, replaces the
inkwell, and returns to his task. This whole scene takes maybe
two or three minutes.

My point here is not to overvalue nostalgic tasks of
days-gone-by, but to point out how far we've come from
that leisurely pace and to call attention to what was going
on in the minds and souls of these people as they lived
these quiet moments of their lives.

As I wandered around my grandfather's farm, I was
learning very important information, not only about my
physical world—land, pigs and, tractors—but about who I
was: "I'm with my grandfather today; he's my mother's
father, he's from Ireland; he talks with a brogue, he loves
horses and pigs; he has a delivery company. I think he likes
to have me with him. . . . " Of course these are not the
words or the awareness that would have occurred to a ten-
year-old boy, but you can be sure I was learning these
things, and much more, too.

The woman shelling peas has spent her time in a kind
of contemplation. As she moved in her soul from her
garden to her neighborhood to her childhood to her sister's
letter, she too was learning important information about
herself: who she is and what she wants. Even the mailman's interruption did not keep her from returning to her
contemplation.

The banker refilling his dry pen sees a metaphor for
himself as the busy executive: He is running dry, needing

to dip into the well of soul, and he refills his reservoir of energy and patience.

These are all moments of Stopping. They are moments of remembering, awareness, and contemplation. My point is that these moments—these life-giving, urgently important moments that slow life down so that we don't miss the important parts—are rare for us now. The good and hopeful news is that we can—and I believe must—make intentional choices to make them happen for ourselves. Because life no longer offers such pauses naturally, we can intentionally create times with little to do and of quiet work. We can place the seemingly blank spaces, the spaces that help us to learn important things, between the events of life. Just as we have had to make specific choices to get sufficient physical exercise, so we now have to make choices to put spaces in our lives, spaces with nothing to do. Creating these spaces is the purpose of Stopping.

Parents can help create safe but unstructured time, time with nothing to do, but with adventuresome space to do it in, for their kids. You might not shell peas, but you probably wash dishes, cut vegetables, mow grass, fold laundry, and do other things. If you don't have a fountain pen to use as a metaphor for refilling your reservoir, you probably have a gas tank. The moments that naturally occur for us are probably not as quiet as they were in years gone by, nor as naturally conducive to contemplation, but that's not a problem. If we first are Stopped enough to notice them, we can change many of those moments from annoyances to life-enhancing opportunities.

Stopping ultimately has the same purpose of intentional living as American naturalist and poet Henry David Thoreau had in 1845 when he went to live at Walden Pond: "I went to the woods because I wanted to live deliberately, to front only the essential facts of life, and see if I could not learn what it had to teach, and not, when I came to die, discover that I had not lived." In the millennial era, most of us can't retire to the woods, so we have to create the Walden moments for ourselves.

Millions of persons long for immortality
who do not know what to do with
themselves on a rainy afternoon.

SUSAN ERTZ

7

Stopping Before Everything

Stopping is a gentle art and is like an encouraging word
that urges us to make the right decisions and choices:
the ones we really want and the ones that are life-giving.
These decisions are both the big, life-changing ones such as
a career change, starting or ending a marriage, or moving to
a new home, as well as the smaller, day-to-day ones such
as, This purchase? That sales pitch at work? Tell her now or
wait 'til later? In both senses of the phrase, Stopping comes
before everything: Stopping should chronologically precede
everything we do as well as assume a position of priority in
our lives.

This is no small adjustment for most of us. This is a
change in direction that will affect all the aspects of our
lives. But I am not afraid that clearly stating the magnitude

of the change will prompt you to say, "This is asking for too great a change. I don't think I want to get into this." I am not afraid to tell the truth because the results are so promising: Not only will you find more moment-to-moment peace, but you will also find clarification of, even the discovery of, your life. Is there anything more important? And could there be anything much worse than knowing—when you are at the end of your life or even at the end of your day—that you missed it?

In both of my fields of work, priesthood and counseling, I have had many occasions to be with people as they are dying. At those moments, the saddest words to hear, and not the least common, are "If only I had known!" or "If only someone had told me!" The implication is that they would have lived their lives very differently and more in line with the truth they now see at the time of their death. And now, of course, they know it's too late. The realization brings a deep sadness.

This has led me to ask myself: Would they *really* have changed if they knew then what they know now? What if someone had revealed the truth to them? Would that have made a difference? My questions remain answerless until I direct them at myself: What do *I* need to know *now* so that I will not be in that situation? Since, as an adult, it is no one's responsibility to tell me what I need to know, what is it that must I tell myself? These are questions that will be answered only in the stillness that allows the hearing of difficult truths and in the slowness that allows me to notice them.

This brings us to another point. It is so obvious that it often escapes our attention. It is this: slowness fosters remembering and speed engenders forgetting. Czech novelist Milan Kundera makes this point eloquently in his novel, *Slowness*. It is a point not only fundamental to the understanding of Stopping, but essential to living successfully in today's world: "There is a secret bond between slowness and memory, between speed and forgetting. Consider this utterly commonplace situation: a man is walking down the street. At a certain moment, he tries to recall something, but the recollection escapes him. Automatically, he slows down. Meanwhile, a person who wants to forget a disagreeable incident he has just lived through starts unconsciously to speed up his pace, as if he were trying to distance himself from a thing still too close to him in time."

Does that ring a bell with you like it did with me? Think of the times when you are trying to remember; you'll notice that you become very still and possibly stare into space. And when we want to forget something? Run, and keep running! Kundera states this truth in the form of equations: "The degree of slowness is directly proportional to the intensity of memory; the degree of speed is directly proportional to the intensity of forgetting."

The faster we go, the more we forget. Then what often happens next is that we forget that we have forgotten. What a state to be in! But when we Stop, we remember again and, therefore, find ourselves.

If you can't meditate, vegetate.

8

Contemporary Contemplation

Stopping is not meditation as it is generally understood. It is a practice intended for citizens of the changing of the centuries who have no time to stop and smell the roses or the time or inclination to practice a whole system of daily meditation. It's for people who don't have time to fit in everything they are already obliged to do, never mind trying to fit in extras like meditating twice a day. Stopping is what I call contemporary contemplation. It is a variety of meditation for those too busy (or maybe moving too fast?) to meditate; it's a way to care for the soul for those who wouldn't otherwise have time.

Stopping is specifically designed for people who are looking for a simple, uncomplicated, non-dogmatic yet effective way to cope with a too-busy life. While respecting and teaching many of the concepts and practices of Eastern (for example Buddhist) systems, Stopping embodies the cultural outlook and customs of the western mind: it's brief, simple to learn, and effective.

From the time I first learned about meditation in my youth to well into the overbusy days of my adult life, meditation has been a challenge for me. It's not that I don't like it; I do. It's not that I have not done it; I have, for some periods of time, with success. I've also read many books on it. Certainly I know that when I do it, I benefit. It's just that I so often find my resistance to meditation stronger than my motivation. It's still hard to get it done. No doubt a simple case of the spirit is willing (but maybe not naturally inclined?) but the flesh is weak (or otherwise ill-adapted?).

Stopping, because it is less structured, works better for me and for many of my clients, although the end results and some of the processes are almost the same as those of meditation. While I still occasionally meditate in a formal, somewhat structured way, I am always Stopping—many times a day, many more times a month, many, many more times a year. I don't find myself resisting Stopping as I do meditation. In fact, I look forward to it.

Perhaps it is a matter of personal preference. The words of Dr. Rachel Naomi Remen, a pioneer in training doctors in relationship-centered care, apply so well here: "I am not much of a meditator," she says in her book *Kitchen Table Wisdom*. "No matter. I have come to suspect that life itself may be a spiritual practice. The process of daily living seems able to refine the quality of our humanity over time." Yes. The intention of Stopping is to help us notice, enrich, and augment "the process of daily living."

One of the purposes of any kind of contemplation is to awaken us, to help us to be in the present moment, so that in the moments ahead we will be on the right track. The word *contemplation* has Latin roots in words that indicate an intensive time spent in the temple to be aware of the signs and omens of the times. Contemplation prepares us for the present moment (and thus for whatever is next) and for what we need to notice now to enjoy success in whatever we are beginning.

I learned the hard way that if I undertook a self-improvement or spiritual project—anything from trying to lose a few pounds or quitting cigarettes to trying to be more patient with a difficult co-worker or less angry and aggressive while driving in traffic—it was doomed to failure if I did not begin the project from a Stopped position. In this way, Stopping is a preparation for the challenges that face us at every turn and even the challenges that we propose and welcome.

The reason why so many of our well-intentioned projects fail is not from a lack of goodwill, not from a failure of willpower or determination, and not from a moral or character weakness. It's that we start these projects from a too-busy, distracted, and unfocused position. It's no wonder they often fail. So Stopping is a first step, a beginning, a prelude. It's the condition we need to be in so that our projects succeed. Beginners are welcome here.

A too-busy, distracted, and unfocused life also kills the power of imagination, an essential part of any healthy life. If we cannot imagine what we dream or passionately desire, we will never be able to realize it. Stopping is a friend of imagination. During a time of Stopping, our imaginations are given space and encouragement to soar.

Stopping is also a primer for some of the more challenging spiritual books and systems that are offered today in such large numbers and various forms. Stopping allows you to be more receptive and positively critical, more frankly understanding or confused, and, ultimately, more successful in whatever you are attracted to adopt and practice.

Stopping can help bring you to the right teacher, can help you recognize your teacher when he or she appears, and can help you to understand that all good teachers should respect your wisdom and shouldn't take themselves too seriously. In that vein, it seems appropriate for to me to say that if Stopping does not do for you what I am saying it can, if it does not bring you into contact with your important questions, and it does not help you to become more awake and remember who you are and what you want, then, of course, you must reject it out of hand.

I am the rest between two notes. . . .

RAINER MARIA RILKE

9

Finding the Spaces
Between the Notes

You'll notice that I quote poets quite a bit. I believe they
are the ones of us who see most clearly. That's because
they are always looking at life. So even though it may
seem that they are difficult to understand (just what does
Walt Whitman mean when he says "I loafe and invite my
soul"?), their vision, once felt, is the clearest we have. So
you will find me quoting people like Frost and Rilke,
Neruda and Angelou, and the ancients, Horace and Cicero,
because they are always looking at life, and looking leads
to seeing what's there. Teilhard De Chardin, priest, paleon-
tologist, and visionary, teaches that "the whole of life lies
in the verb *seeing*." So my goal with the poets is to help us
see what they see.

Poets are the visionaries I turn to when I need to find my way, when I need to see a true and unadorned reflection of myself, or when I need to learn useful skills for my journey. The German poet Rainer Maria Rilke was a passionate and intensely personal poet. In the following poem he gives beautiful expression to the meaning of Stopping. It is from his *Book of Hours, (10)* (translated by Robert Bly):

> *My life is not this steeply sloping hour,*
> *in which you see me hurrying.*
> *Much stands behind me; I stand before it like a tree;*
> *I am only one of my many mouths,*
> *and at that, the one that will be still the soonest.*
>
> *I am the rest between two notes,*
> *which are somehow always in discord*
> *for Death's note wants to climb over—*
> *but in the dark interval, reconciled,*
> *they stay there trembling.*
> > *And the song goes on, beautiful.*

What can we learn from this? In the first stanza, the poet tells us not to mistake his "hurrying," fast-moving life ("steeply sloping hour") for the authentic and deep life that is really his. No. His life is more, so much more, than that.

"Much stands behind me" represents all that he has to keep in his mind, to be aware of, and to remember, and "like a tree," he stands there and embraces it all. In the wonderful line "I am only one of my many mouths," the poet seems to ask us not to be fooled. Of all the things that he has said, only a few are really his. Of all the mouths from which he speaks, only one is authentic, and that one will be the first to be stilled. By death? By intimidation? By wisdom?

He is, he says, "the rest between two notes" of a song. Think of it. Think not of the beautiful, rich tones of the notes. Notes are what we hear, they are the wonderful things of our lives: the events and people. But "Death's note wants to climb over" or dominate, and thus the notes are "somehow always in discord." Without the rest between, without the "dark interval" where values and meanings have their origins, the Death note would win. But it doesn't have to win. During the rest, life happens, value and meaning are given form, the soul deepens its reach, and the song is saved once again. And it goes on being saved again and again and again in all the pauses, long and short, of the song each of us is singing.

The poet asks that we do not define him as the rushing around that we see him doing, but that we should define him as the pause between the events to which and from which we see him rushing; because it is precisely during the pause that the quality of the notes, and his true life, is born.

The poet asks us to be, like him, the rest between the notes: that brief, measured moment between the time when one note of the music stops and another begins. Without that rest, all would be chaotic racket. "Death"— that is, distraction and forgetting—would dominate when

41

all you fill your life with are the notes. All notes and no rests would be Babel. The sound would not be music; it would be more like a siren. But in the "reconciliation" of that "dark interval," the song "goes on, beautiful" because it's there that all the notes become organized and melodic. It is there that they take on meaning and give value.

Here's a practical example for noticing the rests between the notes: You've jumped into your car after dropping off a package at the post office and are on your way to an appointment. You're thinking of what you just did or what you will soon have to do. Dropping off the package and your appointment are your "notes." You do those well. You are busy getting the notes right. But what you likely miss is the right-now, the in-between, the time between the notes, the time in the car when you are going from one thing to another. That's the time I want you to notice. That's the time the poet calls valuable.

Pianist Artur Schnabel, in speaking of his music, makes this point exactly: "The notes I handle no better than many pianists. But the pauses between the notes—ah, that is where art resides!" It is also where the art of living resides and where we transform discordant noise into the music of our lives.

Stopping is taking notice of the space between the notes. Stopping is making the space between the notes important. Stopping is transforming the space between the notes into life-giving waking up and remembering.

Beyond living and dreaming
there is something more important:
waking up.

ANTONIO MACHADO, *Times Alone*
(Translated by Robert Bly)

10

Stopped: Awake and Remembering

Picture a lone traveler on a journey, paused at a fork in
the road, considering the moment, fully awake, poised, not
rushed, aware of his or her power, and, only when the
time is right, choosing the road and continuing the journey.
A decision thus made cannot be wrong. The journey will
be successful, whatever its outcome. The pilgrim is awake
and recalls the answers to the important questions of life.

Now imagine another traveler stumbling down the road,
frantic with anxiety, unfocused, dropping things along the
way, unable to distinguish accurate directions from false
ones, tattered, exhausted and, without thought, taking the
fork in the road that's the closest. Not an appealing model
nor one we would choose to imitate. Yet most of us do.
Racing from thing to thing or from note to note, in a frantic

attempt to keep up or to catch up, we lose our keys, our plane ticket, our date book, ourselves.

Here is an example from my college years: It was at Georgetown University, 1955. So taken up was I with the shouts of "revolt!" that I walked boldly out of class one day with hundreds of freshmen, practically our entire class. I have now forgotten what the intended revolt was about, some perceived inequality no doubt, but we were clearly serious. We had organized the revolt, kept it secret, and then screamed it to the world as we marched onto the football field, daring university officialdom to oppose us.

Then Joe Rock appeared out of nowhere. He was a 250-pound Jesuit priest—most of it belly—with a snarl calculated to induce terror and immediate submission into the heart of any faint-hearted freshman. He lectured us for fifteen minutes with studied gesticulations and barely controlled roars. I can still hear his voice: "There will be no revolt! I'll give you three reasons why there will be no revolt!" Joe Rock always had three reasons for everything even though we were convinced he was thinking up the second and third as he was expounding the first. It was during his "three-reason" lecture that I remembered something: I am not a revolutionary, don't really want to be a revolutionary, and would make a lousy revolutionary.

I had hit the ground running, I had begun this revolt without being awake or mindful. In no way was I Stopped. Neither, it seemed, were my cohorts. We were simply caught up in the heat of the moment. So Joe Rock's posturing easily worked. In fact, I was thinking during his lecture, "He's right, this is silly, this makes no sense at all. . . ." Some revolutionary.

Being awake—knowing who you are—and paying attention to what is going on both inside and outside of you, is close to what the Eastern spiritual traditions call mindfulness. It involves being very present to this moment, to what you are now doing, to this feeling, and to this person in front of you. It is what newspaper columnist Adair Lara means when she relays the story of what her mother wanted on her birthday, "presence not presents." It is noticing the tone of someone's voice and their body language, as well as noticing those things in yourself. It is seeing the many things that occur in your day and quickly establishing whether they are important or trivial. It is tuning in to other people and yourself. Being awake is a very in-the-moment act; an act of right now. It is the opposite of being distracted and unfocused.

Stopping brings you awake and aware of the present moment. But it also helps you bring together the threads of your history, of your stories. It helps you to remember who you are, where you come from, where you are going, and where you want to go; to remember your original goals, ideals, and dreams; and to remember why you started doing what you do so that you can see if that's still what you want to do. Even if you have no clear answers for many of the big questions of life, it is vital to continue to remember what your questions are. Losing your questions is truly losing your way.

Stopping is also remembering in a more literal sense: re-member-ing. That is, to collect again all the parts of you that have been left behind or scattered about in your hurry and to get all your "members" back again into a cohesive whole. The poet Robert Bly speaks of the "bag we drag behind us" as full of those parts that we have lost the use of—our innocence, our spontaneity, or our playfulness. Stopping is reclaiming those parts we did not want to lose, the parts that were stuffed in the bag, maybe years ago, and are hidden and forgotten.

These two gems, awake and remembering, are the essential elements of Stopping.

Carpe diem!

HORACE, *Odes*

11

Stop and *Go for It!*

Stopping is simple to understand. It's a period of time spent doing nothing in order to gain everything. It's taking enough time and creating enough quietude so that you can remember the important questions of your life as well as the current answers that you are bringing to them.

Stopping is a girl sitting in a sun-filled windowseat gently stroking her purring cat, a woman with an open book in her lap gazing out the window and into a distant world, a man walking barefoot along an isolated beach feeling the wind in his face, a driver poised at a stoplight taking a deep breath and relaxing with a soothing thought rather than just wishing for the light to change, a busy nurse taking a one-minute breather and then smiling at her nasty patient, and a salesman mindfully eating his lunch while sitting on a park bench and looking at the sky.

Inherent in Stopping is the idea of creating enough space in your life, whether for thirty seconds or for thirty days, to make sure that you have first things first, that you are not so distracted that you lose the moments of meaning in life, whatever else you might be in the process of gaining.

Notice the definition of Stopping is "Doing nothing as much as possible." "Doing nothing" is a relative term here. Sometimes it will mean not doing much, doing something that takes very little energy, or doing something that you love to do. Paradoxically, doing nothing is doing something very beneficial. Again, Stopping should not be confused with inactivity; life is what it is about.

Stopping is not running from life or avoiding responsibilities. On the contrary, it is moving into life and its responsibilities in a new way. It is having the courage to go precisely where your meanings and values lie and spend time there. Stopping is like an embrace: it holds close and dear those moments which matter the most to you.

Carpe diem seems to be a popular saying these days. I've seen it on tee shirts and it often makes its way into movies. *Carpe diem* means "seize the day" and are the words of Horace, a Roman poet who lived just before the change of the eras (65–8 B.C.E.). *Carpe diem* is an encouragement to take advantage of the time you have. Contemporary equivalents might be "follow your dreams," "don't miss the chances life gives you, you might not get any more," "take a risk." If you really want something, don't let anything get in the way. Have the guts to go for it!

Seize the day. Go for it. Follow your dreams. Take a risk. This encouragement to achieve and get things done was popular in the ancient times of Horace, and we are still quoting him. So what about Stopping in the face of *carpe diem?*—they seem to be at opposite ends of the spectrum. On the one end we have "stop, be quiet, take time to be spiritually awake, and remember the important things" and on the other we have "seize the day, get out and go for it, get what you want, and do it now." Are these mutually exclusive encouragements? Not at all.

I would rather say they differ in sequence of application. In other words, before you seize anything, go for anything, dream, follow, or risk anything, you'd better know what it is you are seizing, going for, or risking. Because we have too much in our lives, we have a tendency to be impulsive, to act before we think—or better—go before we stop. It's like the executive who was so busy climbing the corporate ladder that it was only very near the top that the realization came: The ladder was leaning against the wrong wall. So before we get going, we had better start from a Stopped position or else our going, like my freshman "revolt" at Georgetown, will be inaccurately chosen, poorly carried out, unsuccessfully ended, or all three.

The combination of doing nothing and *carpe diem* is exactly what Stopping is all about. So with apologies to Horace, I say that we had better know what *diem* we want to *carpe* before we *carpe* it, or we are likely to end up with the wrong day. Before you seize the day, stop for a day. Or even for a minute.

II
The
Three Ways
of
Stopping

Finally it has penetrated my thick skull.
This life—this moment—is no
dress rehearsal. This is it!

F. KNEBEL

12

Stillpoints, Stopovers, and Grinding Halts

Stopping has three levels. They are based on length of time: Stillpoints, Stopovers, and Grinding Halts. All are effective, but each one is meant for different moments of life.

A Stillpoint is Stopping quickly and doing nothing for just a moment. It is brief and meant to be used anytime, all the time (every day, in fact), and many times a day. Stillpoints are essentially very short: a few seconds or a few minutes. They are designed to take advantage of the unfilled moments in life: waiting for the microwave to heat your coffee, brushing your teeth, or sitting at a stoplight. They are also to be used at moments of stress: walking into an interview, during a feeling of anger, or when you know you're going to be late for an appointment.

Somewhat less frequent are Stopovers, which are those times that are longer than a Stillpoint, an hour to several days. These are the wonderful times of Stopping, when you really have the feeling that you have been away and have had a mini-vacation for the soul. The most common expression of the Stopover is the afternoon, day, or week-end away, whether you go anywhere or not.

Grinding Halts will probably happen only a couple of times in most people's lives. They are times from a week to a month—or more. Obviously, these need more planning, require a larger and deeper commitment of time and energy, and typically happen at times of life transitions.

These are the three levels, or the three expressions, of Stopping. Each is effective, but the more frequent the repetitions or the longer the time, the more lasting the effect. Think of the three levels as going down (each one deeper and more effective) and plumbing the deeper recesses of your being, allowing you to creatively and joyfully do nothing and to become more fully awake and recollected. These experiences will help you to make accurate decisions and to maintain your true life-direction.

All three expressions of Stopping—Stillpoints, Stopovers, and Grinding Halts—are designed specifically to help you keep one thing in mind: all you have is "now," "then" is gone, and "when" is not yet and may never be.

As the quote at the head of this chapter reminds us, this is not a dress rehearsal for your real life, which will happen sometime later when you are more prepared. You are not waiting for anything to begin; you are in the middle of it.

Except for the point,
the still point,
There would be no dance,
and there is only the dance.

T. S. ELIOT, *Four Quartets*

13

Stillpoints:
The Heart and Soul of Stopping

Stillpoints are the expression of Stopping that can be used most often and that forms the basis, or undergirding, of all Stopping. Stillpoints are quick and focused. Creating Stillpoints during the day is fundamental to the incorporation of Stopping into one's life. They grow by accumulation and thus are the backbone that holds up the structure. A day with fifteen Stillpoints will make you much more peaceful, satisfied, and calm, no matter how much you've had to do, how many people you've had to attend to, or how many fires you've had to put out. Stillpoints also bring you closer to joyful anticipation of the longer Stoppings.

The overwhelming advantage of Stillpoints—especially compared to meditation and other time-consuming systems of quieting—is that they can be incorporated into your life with minimal disruption and maximum effect. You can be with someone constantly for a whole day and that person would never know that during the day you had been renewed and refreshed by fifteen or twenty Stillpoints. I do it all the time:

As I am presenting a seminar to forty nurses, at least ten times during the presentation, I do a Stillpoint. I take a deep breath, focus in, remind myself of what I want to create in this seminar and what I want to offer the participants, and then I go back to what I was doing. This takes a few seconds and the participants experience it only as a brief pause.

Stillpoints are life's little moments of gold that, when taken together, can give brilliance and joy to otherwise dull days. Stillpoints are the little times, brief interludes, quick respites, one minute breaks, breathers, intermissions, and lulls.

But they are also intentional and are chosen for a specific purpose. They, as all Stopping, consist as much as possible of doing nothing and of quietude.

What you do during a Stillpoint is simple: You stop doing whatever you're doing, sit or stand, take a deep breath with your eyes open or closed, focus your attention inward, and remember what you need to remember. Stop,

breathe, and remember. The remembering part is very flexible, it can mean recalling a belief or event that motivates
you. But it can also mean remembering a prayer for
strength or peace, a message you need to hear at the
moment like "you can do it," or a self-encouragement like
"you are okay." Stop, breathe, and remember. Here are
some examples of Stillpoints:

You are on the bus (or train or plane) and are staring
ahead of you, perhaps focusing on the back of the seat in
front of you. You begin by simply noticing your breathing
for a few moments. Then briefly bring to mind some of the
people that are very important to you: parents, children,
spouse or partner, or friends. After a moment or two of
this, simply smile, softly.

You are at the copy machine (or fax machine or on-line
or in line) waiting for it to do what it is supposed to do.
You relax your shoulder muscles, take a slow, deep breath
with your eyes open or closed, and think of one thing for
which you are thankful, for example: "I am so thankful
that I have a friend like Maggie."

The words from T. S. Eliot's poem at the beginning of
the chapter are profoundly fitting for an understanding of
Stillpoints. If it were not for the still point, there would be
no dance. Dancing cannot continue indefinitely. There
must be a point at which the dancing body stops and rests.
It is that point and that time of stillness that gives energy
to the dance, and the dance—life!—is all there is.

So, Stillpoints have a physical part (being still and breathing) and a spiritual part (remembering, praying, thankfulness, or other words that are good for you to hear).

Simple, isn't it? The very essence of Stillpoints is deep, intentional breathing and a moment of quiet recollection. Since breathing is of the essence in Stillpoints, this is a good time to learn the intentional breath.

*"I don't need to know how to breathe,"
you're probably thinking. "I've been doing it since
the day I was born—without a single lesson."*

Ian Jackson

14

Breathing Is Inspiring

I'll never forget the moment I learned to breathe. No, it was not when the doctor slapped my bottom as a welcome into the world and I gulped my first intake of air. It was about forty-five years later when I was in training for certification as an interactive guided image therapist. During one of the sessions, we were led through a breathing exercise. The woman leading the group spoke slowly, calmly, and clearly about the process of breathing and how many of us breathe shallowly.

That teaching changed my life. I don't think anyone around me was aware of it (or were they being polite and discreet?), but as I breathed deeply in and then completely exhaled, involving the entire internal mechanisms of a diaphragmatic breath, I broke into an instant sweat because the experience was so new and overwhelming. As I continued to breathe consciously and fully, I then began to shake, because the experience was so physically and emotionally revolutionary. I know it seems odd now (I must have actually breathed deeply before that?!), but it felt like my first breath and like I had never really breathed deeply before. In the days and weeks that followed, I became a conscious breather, practicing frequently and learning the nuances of breathing.

Conscious breathing means to breathe deeply and intentionally. To breathe deeply is to begin the breath low in your belly and move it up into your chest.

To learn how to do this, begin by placing your left hand over your heart and your right hand over your belly button. As you breathe in, your right hand should move out and away from your body as your lungs fill with air, and your left hand should remain still. This movement should make you look "fatter" than you are; your stomach should be protruding. Then, as you breathe out, or exhale, your right hand should move back towards your body, and your left hand should remain still. The taking in of air moves your stomach, not your chest, out.

Too often what happens is that when we take in a deep breath, the left hand on the chest moves out, meaning that the air is kept shallow and high in the chest and does not bring oxygen to the lungs in an efficient way.

To take this a step farther to an even more complete

breath, begin with your hands placed as above: left hand on your heart and right hand on your belly button. Breathe in and watch your right hand move out. But this time, continue to breathe in and when the right hand is out as far as is comfortable, bring the inhale up to your chest and allow the left hand to move out also. Then, as you breathe out, or exhale, the reverse movement happens as your left hand moves close to the body first and the right hand follows. As you do these breaths in succession, you will see that there is an undulating motion as air moves from down to up and from up to down: from the stomach to the chest and from the chest to the stomach.

That's conscious breathing and it brings several profound benefits: It deepens your awareness of this particular moment and brings you directly into contact with the present. It internally massages the major internal organs, relaxing them, and creates a heightened awareness of yourself and, by its very nature, causes you to expand both spiritually and physically. *Spirit* and *breath* are from the same root; *inspiration* means to breathe in. Breathing is inspiring.

How can I convince you of the power of a deep, intentional breath? Breathing is one of the involuntary activities of the human body, and it seems silly to practice or improve it. But the fact is that many of us breathe shallowly and at times, particularly during stress, we hold our breath so that we scarcely breathe at all. In order to experience the power of intentional breathing, begin by noticing how you breathe, when you hold your breath in and keep it tight (notice this especially when you are concentrating on something or trying to do detailed work) and how it feels when you do a deep, intentional breath.

A wonderful story from the Old Testament applies here. Naaman was a powerful army general who became very ill. He consulted many wise physicians and healers, and none of them could restore his health. Word came to him from a servant girl that Elisha, a wise and powerful prophet in the neighboring country, could cure him. So, in desperation, Naaman and his retinue traveled to Elisha in the distant country. When they found him, Naaman humbly made his request that the prophet use his powers to heal him.

Elisha simply told Naaman to bathe seven times in the Jordan River and he would be healed. The general was infuriated. "We have rivers at home and I bathe in them every day and what possible good could come from simply bathing in a river! This is nonsense. We have wasted our time and effort." Naaman prepared to go. His servants, however, thinking that they had come all this way and that it would do no harm to try, convinced the reluctant general to bathe seven times in the Jordan River. He did so and was immediately cured of his illness.

Like Naaman, we tend to underestimate the power of something that is as ordinary as bathing in the river or breathing in air. Playing the role of Naaman, we might be tempted to say, "Breathing? I've been breathing since the day I was born and I don't suppose I need to learn how to breathe at this point in my life. Besides, how can something so simple and everyday like breathing in and out really make any difference in my life?" I, as your servant, might say, "Well, Your Excellency, you've come all this way, it won't do any harm, and, who knows, it might make a difference. So humor me; why not just try it?"

For now, just trust in the benefits of deep breathing on your physical and emotional state, and, if necessary, just humor me a bit by trying it. Later, you will know for yourself.

You must learn to be still in the midst of activity
and to be vibrantly alive in repose.

INDIRA GANDHI

15

Stillpoints in a Turning World

You now have a clear idea of what Stillpoints are and
you understand the intentional breath, which is its hall-
mark. Now you just have to begin to incorporate them into
your everyday life. Here are some of the ways my clients
and I have found to do that:

A bathroom breather

Yes, the bathroom is one of the best places to go (especially when you don't need to) to take a Stillpoint. "When
everything gets frantic, everyone wanting something from
me, I go to the bathroom," says Eddie, an office manager.
"In my office, the bathroom has a lock, so I lock the door,
look at myself in the mirror, and smile. Then I close my

eyes, relax my body, take a few breaths, and spend maybe thirty seconds in quiet. I end with another smile at myself, maybe an affirmation like 'Take Good Care of Yourself,' splash some cool water on my ears, and go back to work. Total time lapse is two or three minutes. But what a difference it makes about how I feel about work!"

On a scheduled break

Cecilia, a receptionist, explains, "I take a small part of my break, at the beginning, and walk off a ways alone to take a few deep breaths and achieve a moment of quiet. Then I enjoy my tea with the others. The other day my girlfriend asked me what I was doing walking off like that. So I told her. She was so interested, she's trying it now." Sometimes you can use the whole break for this.

Walking from one task to another

"The hospital where I work is huge and I have to cover a large part of it several times a week," says Arnie, a physician. "I am generally alone. The walking is exercise but it is also a time for a Stillpoint, even though I'm moving. Conscious breathing and remembering what matters to me are what I like to do. It does make a difference; especially after a while. If I didn't do this intentionally, I would probably be worrying about what I had to do next or be distracted by my last encounter."

In a tense situation

Have you ever been in a difficult situation, when, for example, you are leading or attending a meeting and someone inappropriately raises his voice or says something mean, unfair, or vulgar? Chances are you tense up, hold your breath, wait for what will come next, and desperately search your brain for something that will fix the situation. After learning Stillpoints, Naomi took a different approach. She trains executives on issues of diversity in the workplace. One day, she faced a sudden, angry, and inappropriate outburst. "The very first thing I did was take a deep breath," she says. "On the second breath, as I inhaled, I imagined the breath coming into me and bringing care, understanding, and love. And then, on exhaling, I directed the breath, with those same energies, through my eyes while I looked directly to the eyes of the man who made the outburst. The effect was immediate. The volatility of the situation was diffused and the conflict could then be resolved later through a normal process."

Notice that in this Stillpoint, the power was in Naomi. It can be in you, too. You can breathe *in* what you need and breathe it *out* where it is needed. The words that Naomi imagined during the second breath were "care, understanding, and love." In the exhalation, the affect of the words were disarming and powerful. You can do this at home when you are about to explode at your child or spouse or after they have exploded at you. As this example shows, Stillpoints are not only a healthy way of taking care of yourself, but they also enable you to treat others better.

When you feel stuck

Try this the next time you are having trouble with some task. Close your eyes for a moment and imagine inhaling the energies of concentration and relaxation. Then open your eyes and, as you breathe out, direct the power of your breath into the task at hand. Repeat this process to build a cycle of moving energy.

Commuting

Often when I am speaking to a group on Stopping, a participant's first personal connection with the idea will be the time spent commuting twice a day. "I call it 'decompression time,'" said one man as he told us what he does to make the transition from work to home. "My commute lasts anywhere from twenty to forty-five minutes, depending on traffic. As soon as I get in my car, my transforming begins. I loosen my tie, put on a relaxing tape—don't listen to the news—and do everything possible to think of my home and my family: how my wife has spent her day and what the kids might be doing. When I finally get there, I move much more easily into the very different world of home."

There are several things you can do to enhance the power of a Stillpoint. You can add a simple, short, self-dialogue or affirmation at the beginning or end of your Stillpoint. Some examples are: "I'm okay, I can handle this," "This will be over soon, probably in a few hours, and I can deal with anything for a few hours,"or "This evening I will take care of myself with a nice _____."

Another good enhancement is to ask, "What would _____ (fill in the name of someone, dead or alive, personally known or not, whom you admire) do in this situation?" Then imagine that you are receiving her or his energy right now, and breathe it into you. Another tool is to visualize the difficult situation you are facing: Close your eyes and "see" it in your mind's eye. In your visualization you make everything go just as you want it to. The rehearsal will lead you in the reality. Many competitive athletes will attest to the effectiveness of this rehearsal visualization.

Please don't underestimate the power of a Stillpoint of even a few seconds. A glance heavenward takes maybe a second and a half, but for you at this time, it can be full of meaning and power because you have already determined its meaning and power. For example, you can say to yourself, "As I glance at the sky (or even at the ceiling), I remember the presence of God in my life and that God's grace is available here and now."

A gesture that is hardly noticed by those around you can empower you in the same way. Here is one I use when I am in a stressful or uncomfortable situation: By simply bringing my thumb and index finger together to make a circle, I remind myself that "This too shall pass." For me it brings comfort, courage, and perspective.

Bernie Siegel, author of *Love, Medicine, and Miracles,* tells of a seriously ill woman who was often overcome by fear. She knew she was in the hands of God, but she would sometimes forget and become fearful. That's when she would merely reach out her hand and, with that gesture, be reminded that she was in God's hands. Her fear would disappear.

The moments of Stillpoints are endless. Search your imagination for yours or for ways in which you need them. These are the times that most accurately correspond to the poet's image of the "rest between the notes." Think of the events of your day as the notes in a song. For the music to be melodious, so that it doesn't sound like a siren, you need to put the pauses in place. During the pause of a Stillpoint, the goal is a period of quiet, of "doing nothing," of being aware of who you are, and of what you want. Then your song "goes on, beautiful."

Spend the afternoon.
You can't take it with you.

ANNIE DILLARD

16

Stopovers: More of a Good Thing

While Stillpoints are the most common, most basic, and most obviously beneficial way of Stopping, the real challenge for most of us is the next deepest level: Stopovers. These are the longer times of doing nothing: an hour or many hours, a day, a weekend, or several days. This is the gourmet fare of the Stopping feast. Even though they are longer in duration, Stopovers are still at the speed of light because they must take place within the context of our fast and full lives.

Stopovers are based on the following principle: It is easier for most of us to take a longer time away from work less frequently than it is to take shorter times off more frequently. For most of us, it is more likely that we will take a full day off every two months or so for a Stopover than to take an hour every day for, say, meditation. Both are good. It's just a question of which you will actually do.

Think of Stopovers as those stations on a long, leisurely train journey where you get off and look around, enjoy the scenery, breathe the fresh air, and return to your journey feeling rested and as if you've experienced a change.

Stopovers are getting away for a while and they have a happy effect: feeling renewed and ready to go again. Jon Kabat-Zinn, a renowned specialist on meditation and stress management, says, "The stopping actually makes the going more vivid, richer, more textured. It helps keep all the things we worry about and feel inadequate about in perspective. It gives us guidance."

One of the necessities of the profession of any family counselor—maybe for your work too—is to be able to maintain the balance between caring deeply about what is happening in your clients' lives without carrying their pain into your own life. An hour-long Stopover is often my way to do this. Sometimes it will happen naturally during the day or, otherwise, I will schedule an hour to be a space between the notes of my clients. I walk mostly, though sometimes I go to a cafe and, accompanied by a cup of tea, watch people.

"My work is very intense," said a woman who supervises a large health care facility. "At work I am always 'on' and when I get home I need time to adjust to this totally different place of family life. So I have a very strict rule: I get to be alone for a half hour before anyone gets any of my time. I think this would be my major Stopping of the day. It's taken a lot of work to make the kids see why I need it, but gradually they have understood."

Stopovers are important for everyone. For most of us, in order to take a significant amount of time for this purpose, our motivation and determination must be strong and clear. Remember the ultimate purpose: to wake up to what is going on in your life, to keep first things first, to remember who you are, and who you want to become, and to remember your ultimate values and meanings. Who can *not* afford Stopovers?

Perhaps the best way for many of us to first experience a Stopover—a longer time away doing nothing—is over a weekend. Pick out a weekend, maybe a few months from now in order to give yourself some time to get used to the idea, mark it on a calendar, and plan an overnight for yourself. Allow the doing nothing part to feel positive to you: "There is really nothing I have to do for a day and a half. No pressure and no expectations at all."

Practically speaking, many Stopovers happen during vacation time. If you vacation with your family, perhaps you could arrange to have a day to yourself and for another member of the family to do the same. On it's own, time off from work is not necessarily Stopping. In fact, many seem to cram their vacation so full and so fast that it defeats its purpose of rest and renewal. So consider a Stopping vacation. It just might be your best vacation ever.

[Going on retreat] has something to do with
an aspect within each one of us . . . unknown
to science . . . that longs to be at peace.

DAVID A. COOPER

17

Stopovers on the Way

The experiences presented here are real Stopovers by real people. The stories were gathered in conversations by phone, letter, e-mail, and fax. They were shared by people who had either read about my work on Stopping or had attended one of my seminars. As you can see, people have been generous in sharing their experiences:

A structured weekend retreat

"I generally don't like most organized retreats," said Barry G. in a phone conversation, "but that was before I discovered a silent, directed retreat. I believe that is what you are calling Stopovers. I was apprehensive as I went for the weekend, all that time with nothing planned and so few people there. A friend had encouraged me to do this when I told him I was often disappointed in retreats, but I was getting cold feet as I arrived. Well, I needn't have. It was wonderful. I can't recommend it enough. I do it now every year because if I don't, I seem to mix things up and have a hard time keeping straight all the things that are going on around me, especially with my family." (See the Kellys' book in the bibliography for information and listings on retreats.)

Your own weekend retreat

You don't have to have a retreat center. One young women, Janet, rented a small, inexpensive motel-type unit in a rural community close to some hiking trails. She spent a weekend alone, roving the hills, eating simply, and resting a lot. "As I think back on it now," Janet said, "I see that it was what you are describing as a Stopover. Of course I didn't think of it that way then. I just did it. I do remember that I didn't tell people what I was doing. I think I would have expected them to think me odd." (See Cooper's book in the bibliography to help you plan your own retreat.)

On a bus

A long-retired school teacher, Howard L., in his eighties, took a three-day bus trip to visit his daughter. He wrote to me: "I didn't plan for this to be a Stopover, but when I read about Stopping in your article, I realized that was exactly what I had done. It was so different. I hardly talked to anyone on the bus, but just remembered a lot of moments and made sure that the few I have left are spent in the right way."

A nighttime reverie

Pam is a nurse. She wrote about her "life-changing Stopping" after attending one of my stress clinics. She spoke of her hospital work in these terms: "Everyone was under a lot of stress and there was a feeling of insecurity and anger. I felt the symptoms of burnout: I dreaded going to work, on my days off I would be thinking about work and not enjoying the day and, worst of all, I would snap at my husband and my one-and-a-half-year-old son. I thought to myself, 'if I am not able to handle this, then I must be a failure.' I was at my breaking point. So, I decided to Stop."

One night, very late, after she returned home from the night shift, she "had had enough! After a good cry I sat at our kitchen table and asked myself 'What is really important to me? What makes me happy?'" Thus passed the hours of Pam's long night, alone at her kitchen table with her questions, the pause between her notes, her dark interval, her Stopover.

And with the dawn? "My number one priority was to be the best mother, and number two was to be a supportive, caring, and understanding wife. Family was more important to me than work. This sounds kind of corny but, in a way, I felt that I had a kind of spiritual awakening that night."

Her Stopover brought about practical changes, too: She put in for a transfer and took a month off to visit her mother, sister, and other family members in Japan. Finally, she added, "I hate to think of what I might be like now if I didn't stop that night."

Just staying home

The busy, type A, executive editor of a small publishing house found that her way of doing a Stopover was to stay put. "Twice now, I have taken a week off and just stayed home—no calls, no visitors, and no going places. I slept a lot, read a little, 'did nothing,' and worked silently in the garden."

A spontaneous opportunity

Soon after she had heard about Stopping, Beatrice, a woman in her forties, called me to say that her Stopover had caught her unaware. "All of a sudden," she said, "I had an appointment canceled and a whole afternoon with absolutely nothing planned. The kids were in school, my husband was out of town, it was a beautiful day, and I had about four hours. Right to the coast I went, to my favorite isolated beach, almost without thinking about it. Like I knew I needed to do this. I was in another space for those hours, and things, at least later in retrospect, became clearer for me."

A birthday gift to yourself

Gerald Reid told of his Stopover in the newspaper. For his birthday, Reid told his wife that he just wanted to spend the day with her and Nathan, their thirteen-year-old son. He wanted them all to do nothing. "But Dad, it's your sixtieth birthday!" his son protested. "You don't even want a present?" "No," responded Reid. He just wanted to spend the whole day completely and exclusively with the two of them. After some resistance from his wife and son, they began to go along with it. His son got into the idea by wishing him "Happy Nothingday, Dad! What do you *not* want today?" They played games (a concession by his wife who doesn't like games), she cooked what he liked, and they talked to each other. He received cards from both of them with messages of love. "Are you going to do nothing next year too, Dad?" his son asked him before bed. Reid asked him why. "Oh, nothing is more fun than I thought it would be," he answered.

A day off for rest and rejuvenation

A recent issue of *Men's Health Magazine* featured an article titled "I Want to Be Alone." Executive editor Joe Kita suggested a day alone filled with healthy pleasures. He acknowledges to his readers that "to spend a day alone, tending to nothing but yourself, probably sounds foreign and even a little shameful." His day's retreat includes silence, hiking, simple food, a nap, exercise, a hot shower, and getting to bed early.

These stories show that Stopovers cover a wide variety of experiences from an hour to several days, from a planned event to a response to one of life's challenges, from a quiet time of insight to a life-changing decision, from a bus ride to a retreat house, and from going some-place different to staying home.

This is a good place to mention the expectations or the hoped-for results you might have of your Stopping experiences, especially of the longer Stopovers. What I want to encourage is that you leave that part open-ended. To have too-specific expectations is often to be disappointed. Part of the gift of Stopping is the discovery of what you were previously unaware of. The ideal attitude to take with you on your Stopover is: "Let's see what happens." What all Stopovers have in common, at their conclusion, is a more awake and aware you.

Prevention is better than cure.

ERASMUS, 1509

18

This Is Your Body Talking

Of course, all of us have probably done Stopovers many times in our lives. But instead of the Stopovers being a conscious choice, they were the result of getting sick. Sickness is often the body's way of talking to us and of getting us to stop when our minds and hearts are so overwhelmed by the challenge of too much that they can no longer get the job done. Not all sickness is this sort, of course, but too much of it is. A sickness-induced Stopover is the body's way of saying, "If you're not going to stop yourself, I will have to force you to stop," and then clobbering you over the head with a two-by-four.

Sicknesses are an ineffective and inefficient way to experience Stopovers. Because you're feeling sick, it's difficult to pay attention and appreciate anything, you're not in a receptive state of mind or expecting any kind of positive goals, and you just lie there feeling awful and waiting for it to be over so you can rise and run again.

I have a friend, Harry, who works long hours and takes little time for himself. One would call him driven. About three times a year he gets sick—the flu or a bad cold—and has to spend a week in bed, hardly capable even of talking or reading, and then he's back to overdrive. Sickness serves him as an enforced Stopover. But it is a detrimental way to do it: He misses most of the benefits and—more important—enjoys none of the pleasure. He only achieves the minimal bodily needs for survival. My hunch is that if he took the same amount of time that he spent sick, one week twice a year, and used it for a scheduled Stopover, he would not only get sick less often, but enjoy life more.

Our bodies speak to us in many different ways. Learning to read your body's language before you become sick is an important result of the cumulative effects of Stopping. You will notice the patterns of sicknesses and identify the various parts of your body that pain you. Stopping encourages you to ask body questions: What is this backache telling me? (Am I "carrying" something I don't want or need to carry?) Why am I always getting a sore throat and cough? (Do I want to voice something that gets stuck in my throat?) Answers to these kinds of questions—even the questions themselves—come in the silence of Stopping, which allows us to notice our current state of health and thus attend to it and prevent many ills.

An excuse is worse and more terrible than a lie;
for an excuse is a lie guarded.

ALEXANDER POPE

19

Excuses, Excuses!

To incorporate Stopovers consciously into one's life, rather than getting sick, is no easy task. It takes determination, clear motivation, and grit because Stopovers involve a significant amount of time. The excuses for not taking the time for Stopovers are endless: too much to do this afternoon; too long away from a spouse, family, job, or sick relative; or too expensive. Excuses are examples of the problem of too much described in part I.

But if you are like me, your biggest fear is yourself. That's what loomed up for me before one of my Stopover experiences, a week's silent retreat. Questions plagued my imagination: What if I find that I am as weak as I fear? What if I remember something horrible that happened to me many years ago? What if—worst of all—as I turn my gaze inward, I find nothing of value there, or nothing much at all? Then what?

The trick in facing my fears was not to avoid these questions but to ask, literally, "Okay, then what? What if I *do* find trouble or even nothing at all when I am Stopped?" "Well," I thought, "then that I had better know it now and see what I can do about it *rather than miss something that needed attention.*" If I needed help, it would be easier to get help now than to wait until I might be too tired and unmotivated. But more than anything, I did not want to miss something vital in the experience of human existence. I wanted to live my life to the fullest, and if there was anything in the way of my becoming all I could be, I needed to know.

It turned out that my retreat was plagued by distractions, chief among them a friend who happened to be close by the retreat house and was recovering from major surgery. Perhaps four times during the week, I went to visit him at the hospital—a serious infraction of the retreat's parameters. So, in the middle of it, I just sort of wrote the retreat off as a good try and let it go, perhaps unconsciously thinking that my worst fears wouldn't even have a chance and I could blame my avoidance on something else—visiting my sick friend. Then, when I was least expecting it, the last two days of the retreat were the most spiritually consoling of my life to that point.

The image that came to me as I was facing my fearful

questions before that silent retreat was an image that was given birth during my high school years: me as a fifty-something-year-old man waking up too early one cold, gray morning and knowing in my deepest soul that I had missed what I most wanted. When I was fifteen, I don't think I could have told you what it was that I most wanted, but I did know that it was urgently vital and that, for me, it was somehow spiritual.

If fears of facing yourself are there for you as you contemplate the possibility of Stopovers, then you are like me and like almost all of us; these fears are natural. I will talk about working with these fears in much more detail in part IV. For now, know that they can be faced—and overcome.

Anyone who incorporates Stopovers into his or her life has given priority to life as a spiritual adventure. If you are reading these words at fifty-something years of age or older, please remember what fifteen-year-olds cannot know: it is literally never too late. Now is the best time to discover who you are and what matters the most to you.

Can you think of a Stopover as an expression of love and an act of kindness to yourself? Indeed it is. But if being loving to yourself is not a good enough reason for you, consider this: A Stopover is an act of generosity for others in your life and for the world at large. A composed and focused soul is a deep richness for all the world, a great gift for those who encounter you, and a desperately needed example in this off-kilter world.

Often the most difficult part of the two-way street of love is the direction that comes toward you. That is, we tend to focus on the giving of kindness and neglect the reality that we also need to receive it. A Stopped person can notice and appreciate the generosities that come his or her way; a rushed, harried, and stressed person cannot. And because love is a two-way street, others observe your qualities of equanimity, calm, and peace, and it gives them not only an example but also permission to explore the same path.

There is a social deterrent to Stopovers. Taking time away from your daily life and responsibilities—whether for an hour, a day, or a week—and, especially, telling people that you are doing it, seems a very unusual or dramatic thing to do and an act which is perhaps more attention-getting than you are used to. It could cause people to talk: from your friends, "How can she leave her family for so long? I wish I could do that," "He must have a lot of money to be away from work so long," or "She's on some kind of retreat? Seems foolish to me, I wonder if she has a drinking problem"; from your kids, "Mom, you're going to be away all that time? Who will cook?" or "Dad, are you feeling all right? Maybe you should just see the doctor"; and from your parents, "Seems like a foolish waste of time, you should be trying to get a better job."

How long should your Stopover be? To get to your answer, follow this recipe: Combine the state of your being, the realistic amount of time you can actually get off, and what you actually feeling like doing at the time; shake them together until the answer presents itself to you. Generally speaking, the longer the better.

Stopovers almost always involve a sacrifice—always of time, sometimes of money—but like any valuable sacrifice, there is good achieved. In this case, the achievement is making sure your whole life is on the course you want it to be on. Not a bad accomplishment for a day's—or a week's—time.

Never swap horses crossing a stream.

AMERICAN PROVERB

20

The Watersheds and Sea Changes of Life

Stillpoints and Stopovers are advantageous for everyone and can be incorporated into life on a day-to-day and week-to-week basis. A Grinding Halt is different. It's an extended time that happens much less frequently, perhaps once or a few times in a lifetime, and may not be needed by everyone. This is not to say that a Grinding Halt is not possible or very beneficial for most of us. It seems, however, to be performed most often by those who see it as a way to resolve some life crisis.

Generally, a Grinding Halt marks a significant life transition or decision. This transition can be termed a watershed, symbolizing a turning point that makes everything flow to a different system, or a sea change, indicating some deep and all-pervasive, but slower, shift of emphasis that has profound and long-lasting effects.

My crisis in the priesthood was a time when a Grinding Halt was needed. My old life made no sense anymore, and I had no idea what the next step should be. Frequently, Grinding Halts are seen as midlife crises because the call to such a transition often comes at midlife, when the pull of spirit is strong.

"Is this all there is to life?" is the question I asked myself before that first and most significant Grinding Halt of my life. The Grinding Halt was the occasion by which I was able to know that I could indeed accomplish some-thing that seemed at the time beyond my capacity: to leave the Catholic priesthood.

At age forty, I found myself pastor of a large parish in Boise. I loved Idaho and had been happily working there as a priest since my ordination in 1963. Suddenly, my midlife crisis hit with a wallop. I was no longer happy or fulfilled by my work in the church. What used to mean a lot to me no longer did, and the positive feelings I valued in the past had changed into doubt and confusion. Even celebrating Mass and leading the Sunday worship services with the parish no longer touched me. Prayer seemed more like work than the joy it once was.

My first coping technique was avoidance. I ran from the parish and school responsibilities, trying to get others to take my place. I became quite good at racquetball and surrounded my daily game with an hour of preparation and an hour of cooling down. This was very different behavior for me. To this point, I had been a hard and enthusiastic worker, bordering from time to time on workaholism. Now I was running from my truth.

My question, "Is this all there is to life?" implied that there must be some other areas of my life that I needed to explore. It was a clear indication to me that the values and meanings of my life to this point no longer moved me. More than anything, that is what scared me. At the same time there were other questions: "Is this merely a stage in my growth as a priest?" and "Is this the time for me to stick it out and buckle down when the going gets tough?" Many wise people advised me in that direction.

I was plagued by questions that brought up anxiety, guilt, fear of loss, and what I might discover: Do I value the celibacy to which I am committed? Does it have meaning for me? Even if it doesn't, have I not promised to live it perpetually? Why am I feeling so alone now when even a year ago I was not? Are the friendships I am now seeking leading me to a more serious kind of relationship? What really is God's will in my life now? What is best for me to do?

I needed to stop. So I did. I was lucky that I could; not everyone can do it as easily. I had a conversation with my well-respected bishop during which he finally asked me, "Dave, are you asking me or telling me that you are going away?" I thought I was asking him; he recognized that I was telling him. If I had to name the force that allowed me to face these questions, I would call it emotional aching over the loss of meaning.

I spent my Grinding Halt, a month, in an isolated town on the northern California coast taking painting classes, which was for me a totally new way to do nothing. That's all I did. I made no friends and kept to myself. My questions, which now were not so demanding, faded into the background. I felt like my internal computer was scanning all my files, moments, facts, and feelings of my existence up to that point and that this scanning was going on all the time as part of my autonomic nervous system; it was out of my conscious control.

The purpose of the scanning was to ensure I didn't forget any necessary element as I made a possibly life-changing decision. The quiet was to assure that I was not too distracted by life for the scanning to take place. In the meantime, what I was externally doing was trying to mix pigments to capture the unique green of the cypress found on the California coast and creating a beginner's bunch of watercolor paintings of that stunning and scenic coast.

By the end of my stay, the scanning was finished. I returned to my pastoral responsibilities for one year, at the end of which I made my decision. I left my position, returned to school, earned my degree and psychotherapy license, and began a new life as a family therapist. This, indeed, was a watershed moment: a dividing line that will continue to serve as a major point of transition in the course of my life.

As I reflect on this experience, I realize that my Grinding Halt would not have been possible—I just would not have had the power to get it done—without having in some way, years before, incorporated what I now call Stillpoints into my life. It was the accumulation of those moments that gave me the courage to do what I had to do at that moment of pressure and that moral crunch. It was a life-changing decision that involved disappointing a lot of people, breaking vows that I had taken to God and to the world, and violating long-standing family rules, as well as, taking a risk to find out if I could personally carry it off and make it in the world.

I can't say that my transition was without problems, regrets, or pain. I can say that I know it would have been much worse—more messy and more hurtful to myself and others—without the Grinding Halt. I can also say that at every stage of the transition, I had a sense that I was at least minimally aware of all the elements that were in play for me. And it has been a happy decision, thanks to Stopping.

During major transitions, the influence of the spiritual is a strong, almost magnetic force, because these major changes always involve our values and meanings of life. In the course of the change we are rightly concerned that we may lose them. Soon after I left the priesthood, a thoughtful woman in my parish sent me a small holy card, which, sadly, I have misplaced over the years. But I remember clearly the idea of the words on the card: Don't lose the ideals that have safely brought you this far. Receiving it was one of life's little gifts. I hope one day I will be browsing a long-unopened volume and will come upon her holy card.

What are your watershed moments? What are the sea changes in the ocean of your life? Are you in one now? Is one looming on the horizon? Maybe it's time for a Grinding Halt. And, if not now, chances are that there will be one sometime in your future.

No retreat. No retreat.
They must conquer or die
who've no retreat.

JOHN GAY

21

Grinding Halts Are Good for You

The need for Grinding Halts indicates that something big
is going on. They are often needed, as in my case, to avoid
some undesired result. As the epigraph above indicates, if
we do not have a way to retreat or to get away for a while
in order to allow some as-yet-unavailable idea or power to
present itself, the only possibilities seem to be waging war
or death. Grinding Halts give us the productive time to
arrive at a healthy alternative. The alternatives don't have
to be as dramatic as a complete career change, and they can
happen in any number of ways. Here are a few:

An island sojourn

Several years ago, in the spring and after months of
planning, I rented a simple, one-room cabin on Lopez

Island in the middle of Puget Sound off the coast of Washington. I arranged this trip so that everyone knew well ahead of time that I would be gone and that only emergencies would justify a phone call. I brought only one book and a journal. I had a bicycle and sufficient food for myself. I walked a lot, bicycled, read a little, wrote a little, meditated twice a day, and spent most of the day basically supporting life and doing nothing—just being. I rarely talked to anyone and, for a few days, spoke to no one at all. For two weeks, I just was.

I chose this way to do a Grinding Halt for several reasons. I had already done a week-long, silent retreat and wanted something different and longer. Also, I felt an allurement to that part of the world and to life on an island in a remote setting. It was a place where my soul felt at home.

I did it at that time because it was a moment of transition in my life and I wanted to be as awake as I could be so that I would make the right decision. Should I leave the social service agency where I was working as a family counselor and take the leap into private practice? Many of my old doubts came back to plague me: Could I do it? Wouldn't it be safer and wiser to stay with something secure but limited rather than go out and take a risk?

Once back from the island, my confidence seemed to take over and I opted for the risk. My transition succeeded. Would it have done so without a Grinding Halt? I don't think so.

To answer why, let me again use the computer as a metaphor. As I understand it, a computer constantly scans numerous bits of information, all in the form of a series of ones and zeros, and gathers only what it needs to do the requested task. That's what happens during a time of a Grinding Halt. Your internal computer scans your life, all that has gone before, all the paths you have trod, all the teachings you have received, and all your values and meanings of life. The hallmarks of the Grinding Halt are the acts of noticing them, counting them, and saying to them, "Yes, I have noted you. I am aware of you. I have taken you into account as I make my decisions for the future." Some of this scanning is quite conscious and deliberate, but most of it is unconscious and automatic. It happens as you ride your bike, cook your meals, and gaze at the sea.

A nine-day retreat

Sally is a married woman in her mid-thirties, a mother of two, a part-time teacher, and a frequent volunteer at her church. She decided that life had become overwhelming. It wasn't that she was particularly unhappy—in fact her life was on the surface very satisfactory—but she was "becoming emotionally numb, not really giving attention to what I wanted to give attention, and even when I did, it was like I was someone else doing it. I felt a stage removed from myself."

Her Grinding Halt took the form of nine days of silence and quiet at a retreat facility just a few miles from her home. Her biggest challenge was her husband and friends. She took the time and energy to explain what was going on and how important this was for her well-being and her family. Reluctant at first, her husband supported her and later did his own form of Stopping. Her friends came around only after she had returned.

"One friend still thinks it's a bit silly, that it's fine if you're old and retired and have nothing else to do," Sally says, "but now, I don't care if people don't like it. I know how important it is for me. I can't wait to do it again, maybe in a few years, and for an even longer time."

"It's difficult to explain exactly what I got out of it," she said, "but I can say that I felt more confident that I knew myself better, that I had somehow strengthened my relationship with God, and that whatever I did from now on, I would not feel so isolated or abstracted from life."

Sally's experience came at a moment of spiritual crisis and at a turning point in her life. Notice her major transition was not a dramatic rupture of life events nor an emotional upheaval. This was a sea change kind of transition: slow and quiet.

Time alone in the mountains

Jeffrey is an graduate student in his late twenties with teaching-assistant duties, a serious girlfriend, and part-time work. "Frazzled, totally stressed out," he described himself at the time. "I had very little money and absolutely no time at all." But he did have "two large decisions" facing him "involving love and work." He also had an old car, some camping equipment, and a strong desire to be awake spiritually.

He put together a Grinding Halt for himself that took some coordinating but was worth the work. He planned it around spring break, spent a few months saving money for missed work, and got the encouragement of his girlfriend ("She thought it was a great idea," he said, "she knew I needed it.") He spent twelve days at a secluded campground, living in his tent.

"I read my sacred writings, hiked, kept notes, cooked on my camp stove, and changed my life," he said. "When I'm sixty, I'll forget a lot about these years, but I know I'll always remember that time alone in the mountains."

Around the world

Ann had worked her way up to marketing director in a small company. She had graduated from a prestigious college and through mentoring, native intelligence, and experience had gained wisdom that was at least equal to a graduate degree. She was doing very well. Then, just like that, she quit. She spent three months traveling the world, working as she went, "to get in touch with herself." When she returned, she got work as a marketing director for one of the biggest companies in her field. Her Grinding Halt brought her clarity and, ultimately, a better position.

Canceled workshop

Susan tells of her unexpected experience of a three-week Grinding Halt. "The instructor became ill and a long-anticipated workshop was canceled. I was on a small island—a mile by a mile and a half—off the coast of Maine, so I just stayed there. At the time I was mad at my boyfriend who went to Europe without me, so it was a weird context. But what happened for me is that the power of nature took over. It was incredible. I was by myself, and yet I was with nature." She wandered the island and visited the many artists there, looking at their work. "I noticed the weather change, from cloudy to cold to sunny. My body rhythms and the rhythms of nature became my clocks."

As with many, Susan's Grinding Halt led her to appreciate the natural world. Think for a moment of what she did: three weeks essentially alone while wandering around a small island and being aware of the changes and rhythms, subtle and dramatic, of the natural world.

Illness and death

Sometimes Stopping is in response to a life event that is overwhelming. Barbara is a fifty-nine year old woman who had been married thirty-seven years and had one child, a thirty-five-year-old married daughter. She wrote to me, "Three years ago my husband, Jerry, became quite ill and, after five miserable months of doctors and tests, was found to be HIV positive. Three days later he was hospitalized with PCP (Pneumocystis carinii pneumonia)—an AIDS

diagnosis. Five days after that, I found I was also HIV positive. Jerry recovered slowly from the pneumonia only to
fall ill again and again until he died a year and a half ago."

Soon after her husband's diagnosis and after several
attempts to find an appropriate counselor, she found an
understanding and helpful priest. "I remember saying to
him at my first visit that I wanted more but I really
couldn't say what it was I wanted more of! My future
seemed to open before me like a black abyss—and I was
very much afraid." She decided to do something about it.

"My husband's religious tradition has rather elaborate
funeral services including a forty-day memorial service.
Right after that, I retreated. I closed myself off from as
much of the world as possible. My daughter brought me
groceries. I went nowhere but church. Six weeks after his
death, family and friends began to get on with their lives,
and I was left to my own devices, as it were. During this
time I was not lonely. I had plenty of time to read, ponder
and mind-wander, meditate, experience, and work
through various stages of grief and pain.

"Surprisingly what came out of all this was the most
marvelous enlightenment of one very pure, simple fact:
God loves me unconditionally! My whole life had changed.
My focus was crystal clear.

"I firmly believe if I had not had this opportunity of
Stopping when I did, this great revelation, this enormous
gift from God, would not have come into my life. I was

able to open myself to it not even consciously knowing what I was doing or why. How long has this been going on inside my soul?

"Now I feel my life is just beginning. Wonderful things have happened and doors have opened."

So, what are you wondering about Grinding Halts? Are you drawn to the idea? Or maybe you are put off by it? Perhaps just somewhat neutral? Maybe you have, in fact, already done a Grinding Halt. If you are drawn to do one, then things will take care of themselves and you probably will. If you are put off or neutral toward the idea, my request is only that you remain open so that if you become aware of the need for a Grinding Halt, you won't miss it. You'll recognize what you need and be able to respond.

The way to do is to be.

LAO-TZU

22

Growing "Like Corn in the Night"

Just how does Stopping—whether Stillpoints, Stop-overs, or Grinding Halts—work? Earlier I used the meta-phor of a computer and the internal scanning that it does. When we are Stopped, the scanning happens on its own; we give ourselves time for anything that needs attention on some level of our consciousness. The fascinating thing about the process is that it does not have to be conscious. You don't have to analyze your way out of anything. All you have to do is put some space and time around your-self, and your marvelous mind and soul will sort it out.

Henry David Thoreau has another, more earthy image to tell us how we grow during Stopping. Here are his words from *Walden*, which could well be described as the key American document from the 1840s, to support the

Stopping I am encouraging a hundred and fifty years later.

First, he describes one of the wonderful moments of his two-year experiment of living alone at Walden Pond in Massachusetts in order to "live deliberately" and awake:

"I sat in my sunny doorway from sunrise till noon, rapt in a reverie, amidst the pines and hickories and sumachs, in undisturbed solitude and stillness, while the birds sang around or flitted noiseless through the house, until by the sun falling in at my west window . . . I was reminded of the lapse of time."

This is a wonderful description of a contemplative kind of Stopover: "from sunrise till noon, rapt in a reverie."

Then he tells us how he grew:

"I grew in those seasons like corn in the night, and they were far better than any work of the hands would have been. They were not time subtracted from my life, but so much over and above my usual allowance. . . . I minded not how the hours went . . . it was morning, and lo, now it is evening and nothing memorable is accomplished. . . . I silently smiled at my incessant good fortune."

"Like corn in the night" is a wonderful image that is full of power. Can you place yourself inside a cornstalk on a moonless night? Can you imagine being inside the growing ear, absorbing the nutrients from the earth, having retained in your flesh the warmth of the day's blazing sun, drinking in the moisture of the dew, and combining it all to create the miracle of the bright, yellow food? That's how we grow when we're Stopped. It happens on its own, we don't have to *do* anything.

To search out the deep truth of life,
to lift a veil from its fascinating secrets . . .

MARIA MONTESSORI

23

Freeing and Finding Your Truth

I hope that by now you see that Stopping—in all its forms—works because it allows for and facilitates truth, your truth, to have its way. In fact Stopping can't fail; it can't be wrong because there is nothing to be wrong or right—no content, no doctrines, no dogma, no beliefs, and no system of adherence—only a clearing away of whatever is cluttering up your truth. And when your truth is freed, identified, and given wings, your life will be enhanced, deepened, and enriched. So Stopping is a way, a very simple way, to get to your truth.

I want to encourage the freeing of truth that is most essentially *you*, the identification and answering of *your* calling, because I believe that is the most important accomplishment in life, and that is how you most clearly discover and develop the values and meanings of your life.

What you encounter during Stopping will be unique to you. It is also noble, worthy, and life-enhancing, even though it can bring to consciousness painful or difficult issues. The most significant fact is (oh, what a different world it would be if we all believed this truth!) *there is nothing wrong with you.* An important goal of Stopping is knowing that fact, not hoping that it might be true, not thinking that it is sometimes true, but knowing that there is nothing wrong with you on many different levels: through knowledge, facts, and feelings in your mind, in your body, in your heart, and in your soul. And this is true even though you (like most of us) can think of many areas where you need improvement: times when you are less than wonderful and even moments when you are down-right terrible. Those are things that show that you are human, that you are not God.. There is nothing wrong with you! (If this is a sticky point, see Cheri Huber's book in the bibliography for help.)

But Stopping also involves another dimension of encountering truth, one that balances and fulfills the process of freeing. It is *finding* your truth. By that I mean the need we all have to get out of our own way, to get over ourselves, to go out from ourselves, and to find that *something else* that adds a special dimension to life.

The ultimate goal in finding truth is discovering one's purpose or calling. They are blessed who know, at least to some degree, the primary reason for their existence and the answers to, "Why am I here?" But equally blessed—if not more so—are those who are aware of the questions and are attentively searching for the answers, even if their attainment is ultimately illusive. It is precisely in the searching wherein lies our nobility. Stopping's purpose is to serve the search.

So Stopping can't go wrong even if it brings challenges and pain and messes. Much more likely to go wrong are the projects and plans you undertake before you are ready to undertake them and the search for purpose that will lead you far in the wrong direction because you are inattentive—before you are Stopped. And, perhaps more to the point, what will likely go wrong are the valuable projects and plans you will never undertake because you are not Stopped enough even to recognize them.

When you are actively engaged in both processes, freeing your truth and finding your truth, then life—no matter how frantic—is right.

We must find some spiritual basis for living,
else we die.

BILL WILSON

24

Everyday Spirituality

At this point it is evident that Stopping is essentially a spiritual process. *Spirituality* is a challenging word. Many folks don't like it because it is too general, bland, and loaded with so many meanings that it can end up meaning nothing. Ernest Kurtz and Katherine Ketcham ask, "What is spirituality?" in their book *Spirituality of Imperfection.* They say, "to have the answer is to have misunderstood the question," precisely because it can mean so many different things. While acknowledging this problem, I have been unable to find a satisfactory substitute for the word. So rather than throw it out, I have formed a broad, working definition based on a description by theologian David Griffin and on an idea from psychologist James Hillman:

"Spirituality is the ultimate meanings and values by which we live our lives, both on the peaks and in the vales."

That is, spirituality consists of what we sacrifice for, what we put first, and what we would let go of last. It is our answers to the big questions of life, and it is our deathbed truths. It is the meanings and values that influence how we live from day to day, from decade to decade, and for a lifetime. Our morality is based on our spirituality; the rightness or wrongness of how we understand our actions is based on what we value and where we find meaning.

I like to call this definition *everyday spirituality* because it is useful for the speeded-up kind of lives we actually live. Everday spirituality is accessible for literally everyone, all the time: for those within a belief system or religious affiliation with very otherworldly values, and for those who, without such a system, hold very worldly values, or any combination of the two. This allows a wide range: from the strict orthodoxy of an ancient, organized religion to a personally created system that involves music, reading, exercise, and volunteerism to any combination thereof. God will not be limited. Grace knows no bounds. For those with the eyes to see, everything is sacred.

The second part of the definition has to do with the use of the words *soul* and *spirit* and I can think of no better way to understand their differences than by using the metaphor of James Hillman: peaks and vales.

Hillman identifies *soul* as residing in the vales, the low, fertile valleys of human experience. "Soul is always tethered to life in the world," says psychologist and best-selling author Thomas Moore, commenting on Hillman's idea. "It can't be separated from the body, from family, from the immediate context, from mortality." Soul can often be messy and dark. Soul is what grounds us to the world; it gives warmth and moisture to life and to our meaningful relationships with other people.

Spirit, on the other hand, tends "to transcend these limitations of the valley," notes Moore. Spirit focuses on the "afterlife, cosmic issues, idealistic values and hopes." It resides in the higher, drier, and more airy peaks in the sky. Its focus is transcendence—clearing the limits of the body and the other darker, messier tendencies of human nature.

But—and here is the point I want to emphasize—when the spiritual transcends the earthiness of the soulful to the point where it becomes split off from the soul and receives no influence from it, the resulting spirituality readily "falls into extremes of literalism and destructive fanaticism," as Moore notes. So a spirituality that separates spirit from soul will lead to only half the truth, to serious one-sidedness, and to deep trouble.

When I use the words "spirit, spiritual, and spirituality," I include both the peaks (transcendent and selfless aspirations) and the valleys (earthly struggles of delight, confusions, and muddling through); both the crisp, silent, clarity of a moment of isolated and absorbed contemplation and the experience of intense erotic pleasure with your beloved; and both the isolated monk disciplining his human nature in order to achieve a higher union with God and the mother who, with love and humor, handles way too many messes in the valley of family life.

I shall never forget a hallowed moment in my life that included both spirit and soul. I was sixteen and was on a canoe trip with a dozen other kids and our guides in the lake-studded wilderness of northern Ontario. We had made camp early that day and chores were done. It was the time between evening and night which at those northern latitudes is so blessed with a unique and amazing light. I took a canoe out on the lake, alone.

For some reason I stopped (yes, Stopped!) in the middle of the lake and lay down in the bottom of the canoe and kept very still. I heard (I can hear it now!) the water gently lapping at the sides of the boat, the faint, occasional sounds of my follow campers talking and laughing far in the distance, and the silly laugh of a loon at the other end of the lake. I saw only blue-gray-rose sky. I felt the coolness of the water against my back through the canvas skin of the canoe as well as the hardness of the canoe's wooden ribs. At that moment I knew something utterly important— even though it is still most challenging to put it into words. It was something like: everything is right and I am part of it. I feel profound gratitude for that moment.

As is often the case, that transcendent peak was quickly transformed into a messy valley. I paddled quietly back and, as I was arriving at our camp, the guide began to yell at me, "Never do that! That is a very stupid thing to do! You should know better!" An empty canoe in the middle of a lake, he explained to me, is an immediate alarm signal for anyone seeing it. Of course, I knew right away what he meant. He saw me leave and, at some point, he happened to look out and saw only what appeared to be an empty canoe and no me. But I hadn't thought of that.

A moment on the peak, a lesson in the valley; both are necessary and holy.

The other point to remember about spirituality, as Kurtz and Ketcham point out, is that we all are spiritual whether or not we are religious or call ourselves spiritual. We all have values and meanings by which we live our lives, in the valleys and on the peaks, whether they are examined or ignored. In this sense, spirituality is like health. We all have health, well or ill or attended or neglected. So with spirituality. The important question is not whether we have a spirituality or not but whether our spirituality is leading us to integration, knowledge, and wholeness or not.

Often spirituality and religion are confused. Religion is the form or structure, which at its best fosters and feeds human spirituality and at its worst kills it. Spirituality, however, is a process of maturation toward the fulfillment of your meanings and values, which lives outside as well as inside religion.

I believe it is good for everyone to have a specific spiritual practice. That is, a way composed of specific teachers, events, rituals, moments, habits, customs, readings, sayings, doings, works of service, traditions, celebrations, icons, works of art, artistic expressions, places, spaces, times, symbols, words, images, sounds, colors, acts of kindness, and so on, almost endlessly, or any number of these in any combination

Having a spiritual practice is important for at least two reasons. First, it acknowledges that you are living both on the peaks and in the valleys and that you have desire and grace not only for the peaks, but also the humility, humor, and practical helps for the valleys. Having a practice encourages your spirituality to be useful; it supports an everyday spirituality.

And second, because it will help you in your Stopping; Stopping is essentially spiritual—that is, it deals with meanings and values. If you already have a spiritual practice as you cultivate Stopping into a habit, you won't be unprepared for its results. You will have ways that you have developed to process and develop your Stopping experiences.

Imagine having an important insight about yourself: maybe a new way of seeing that you are more seriously dedicated to serving the needs of people than you previously realized or that you are more deeply passionate about learning the cello than even you suspected. Now imagine not knowing what to do with these insights that are the spiritual gifts of Stopping. With a spiritual practice in place, you can go to your readings, your prayers, your sacraments, your trusted guide, your service work, your music, or whatever makes up your practice and use it as a way to process the gifts and, therefore, as a way that leads you to integration. Thus the gifts of Stopping are not lost or missed, but developed and enjoyed.

With Stopping, I want especially to access your deeply felt desires to feel less stress, to make better decisions, to be a better parent, friend, and co-worker, to feel more organized and efficient, and especially to experience joy. No, that's not quite right. What I really want is to lead *you* to access those same desires of your heart. I want you to access the desires that are too often blocked and frustrated by poverty—of pocketbook and spirit—by fear, or, even, by the churches and institutions that should be the very connectors.

I believe all deep and yearning desire is in some way a wish for integration and unity with the world and, ultimately, with God or however you define the divine reality for yourself. From elegant corporate boardrooms to raucous and mean streets, there is not much difference in the aching desires in the hearts of people. Even the addictive covers of these desires are similar—money, power, cocaine, alcohol, crime, violence, apathy, and boredom—although the styles are often different. Beneath these painful expressions is a hidden, noble, indeed a divine, yearning.

Stopping is designed to connect you to your heart's

desire and to help you identify it, name it, pursue it, and realize it. It does this by giving you the opportunity to be quiet enough, often enough, to hear your own wisdom. In fact, it isn't really the Stopping that will do it; it is you. Stopping can help you get to the point where you recognize your own wonders.

There's no guarantee, but this is the best chance we've got.

III

The Gifts
of
Stopping

I lean and loafe at my ease . . .
observing a spear of summer grass.

WALT WHITMAN, *Leaves of Grass*

25

Stopping's Benefits

Stopping is a rich and multifaceted experience, somewhat like having lived in a wonderful old mansion for
many years and then one day discovering a whole new
wing with new rooms full of wonderful things. We are that
big, old house, and we have some wonderful rooms waiting for discovery and exploration.

The Stopped person enjoys many different benefits, best
described as the gifts of Stopping. Like the rooms in the
mansion, they've always been there, but we've been too
busy to explore them. Fully discovering the beneficial gifts
of Stopping is something like walking through the newly
discovered wing, opening each of the doors, and spending
some time in the rooms.

I have tried to choose the most important of Stopping's gifts or traits to look at, the benefits that get most closely to its heart. Surely there are more; every Stopping experience will be proof of that. But these seven seem to be essential:

Capacity for paying *Attention*; achieving true *Relaxation*; knowing and enjoying *Solitude*; *Openness* to what is, as it is; forming strong but flexible *Boundaries*; embracing your *Shadow*; and identifying and living out your *Purpose*.

These are the gifts that Stopping offers those who embrace it. They are gifts that are sometimes discovered for the first time, are more often rediscovered after being lost or misplaced, and are most often already present and in need of appreciation. Stopping develops and encourages these gifts into new levels of excellence and enjoyment.

Let's look at each gift—one by one—along with some suggestions for how to encourage them.

Someone sold us out—but only
when we ceased to pay attention.

TIMOTHY FINDLEY, *The Telling of Lies*

26

The Gift of Attention

Being awake and remembering is the gift of paying
attention. With this gift, we are encouraged to notice what
is within us, what is important to us, and what is attrac-
tive to us. As Stillpoints are the heart and soul of the
expressions of Stopping, so paying attention is the heart
and soul of the gifts of Stopping: it forms its very soul and
nothing gets more directly to its heart. It is the trait that
defines the Stopped person as aware of what is going on
right now and remembering all that's important and
meaningful to him or her. Attentiveness is similar to the
concept of mindfulness that is so important in the Eastern
spiritual traditions.

Distractions are the archenemy of attention. Many of us
are so busy, so overwhelmed, and thus so spiritually asleep

that life can consist of mindlessly moving from one distraction to another: get up, eat breakfast, rush to work, work all day, go home, eat, watch TV, and go to bed. In such a day, you can never once be really awake or know and feel why you are doing this routine over and over or even if you really want to do it. Or maybe your whole day is spent focused on others: your kids, spouse, customers, clients, or boss. Time for yourself is squeezed in, hardly remembered, and haphazard. Losing track of time and date is a sign of distractedness.

In such a state we are simply moved by whatever happens to be loudest or most demanding at the moment. Not that our pursuits are without importance or value, but if we are not present to them or aware of what we are doing or why we are doing them, at least to a degree, then we are distracted.

By distraction, I also mean anything that takes your mind- or soul-attention, off what it wants to be on. Distractions are often trivial and demand your attention as if they were important or meaningful. This causes you to put last things first or the cart before the horse. Literally, you're off track, you're dis-tracked.

Anything that tells a lie about itself in order to get your attention is also a distraction. Some advertising is a great example of distraction. The ad says, "this is important, this is true," and it often makes these statements about precisely what is *not* important and *not* true. It often lies and perhaps even more amazingly, it insults us, assuming that we are not aware that it is lying. We have grown accustomed to it, which makes it even more powerful. Listen to these: "Make a more wonderful you" by using this soap, "Be at the top" by buying this car, and "Life is worth" this brand of crystal. As if soap could make you more wonderful or driving any kind of car would put you on the top of anything worthwhile. And if life is worth a particular kind of crystal, then life is also worth smashing it to bits. If we are attentive, we have knowledge of our wonders, of what we want to be on top of, and of what is worthy in life. If we are not attentive, we could have the tragic fate of being guided through life by the advertisers of Madison Avenue.

Just yesterday I heard on the radio that wearing a particular brand of eyeglasses "will tell the world who you are." "No, it won't!" I answered the lying ad out loud. "But Stopping can!"

Dis-tracked, we pay attention to what is not life-giving, helpful, healthy, enjoyable, nor important, while we hope whatever we are focused on will be all those things for us. Distracted, we miss the important moments. They pass us by and we don't even notice: a phone call from an old friend, a momentary view of the rising full moon through the dark trees, a remark or a question from a child, or the light and color of an autumn evening—all missed, untapped, unused, and lost. Nor do we even notice that we did not notice.

It is difficult to categorize distractions because almost anything can become a distraction and almost anything can be made noble. It has to do with being awake. An attentive person can say to a distraction, "You are a lie and I give you no importance and no influence in my life." The key question is always, "What is really going on here? What is the truth of this situation?"

Picture a person who goes from a sterile marriage to boring work, goes back home to an evening of stultifying television, and starts all over again the next day. A sad existence. However, a person with a different attitude who is married, who works, and who watches television can have a life that is richly meaningful. We must tell ourselves constantly: "Wake Up! Pay attention! What is really going on here?"

Stopping allows us to pay the necessary attention in order to prioritize life. In this way, Stopping is like the death of a friend. It leads us to value and appreciate every moment of our own existence as priceless and irreplaceable. We can ask the long questions and the big questions: "Am I doing what I really want to do?"

That was my challenge several years ago when my friend Bill died of AIDS. I have been filled with so many feelings from the moment he told me of his illness to the moment I am writing this: anger (yes, I was mad at him for getting sick); love; empathy; appreciation for his good example, expressed friendship, and engaging sense of humor; frustration at not being able to do anything; and so many more feelings.

But what ultimately came out of my experience with Bill was the determination to be attentive to my life. His death reminded me in a very intimate way that life is short, often difficult, unpredictable, of limitless value, and has parts of it that are important to me and others that are not. So I should get it all in order right now. Tomorrow? Who can count on that?

Forgetting follows directly from distraction. We forget where we came from, how we came from there, where we are going, and why we are going there. We forget our values and the ancient rituals that ground us and tell us who we are.

Two years ago my oldest brother gave our family a wonderful gift. He encouraged and supported his son-in-law to research, write, and publish a book on our paternal grandfather, Theodor Kundtz, who had come to the United States from Hungary as a penniless boy and became one of the memorable citizens of Cleveland. His story is a wild ride with all the ups and downs of a true saga.

But more than that, what this book did for our family was to present all of us with a great many moments of remembering ourselves. Some of the stories were familiar to us, but many stories were newly heard; "I never knew that . . ." was a common comment. Now we know more about ourselves because we remember where we came from and how we are here in this place and time; our story is enriched. We can enjoy ritual moments of pointing to photos and saying, "That's the boat he came over on" and

"That's Uncle Joe. He died before I was born." As members of our family pick up this book and browse, we are given many moments of Stopping.

When we are inattentive, we can forget what is truly valuable. We all enjoy getting a new piece of sporting gear or a new gadget for the kitchen. But in the long run, a new tennis racket or a new blender probably means nothing really important. A tennis racket can bring you some pleasure and perhaps help your game; it cannot make *you* better or happier. It's an easy slide from "the prestige of ownership" to believing that you are now more fulfilled and are somehow better.

However, to keep balance, we must not miss the beautiful soulfulness of the things of the world. The same tennis racket and blender can indeed help bring to our lives valuable qualities that enhance our moments both on the peaks and in the valleys. As always, it's a question of balance and of meaning and value.

When we are distracted and forget what is true and important for us, we tend to make mistakes: I forget appointments, I bring the wrong book to the meeting, or I know the correct size of the battery I need but I buy the wrong one. When we go without Stopping, the chances of making a mistake along the way are high.

When I think of paying attention, I think of the words of Sister Mary Odillo, my seventh-grade teacher. She would say to me (too often), "David, stop daydreaming and pay attention!" She was right, of course; I did have to learn arithmetic. But I—and every other kid sitting in a schoolroom and daydreaming on a spring afternoon—was also right; there was a lot of important stuff I *was* paying attention to as I was daydreaming. The trick is to hit the balance between daydreaming and long division.

Being attentive is about noticing. I really like the word *noticing*. It implies so much. It has a lack of urgency and a quietness about it. When we notice things or moments, we take them in, consider them, and note them. They become ours not in a grabbing kind of way, but in a friendly and useful way. As I reflect on this past week, I *notice* some moments: a very small girl, seated in a grocery cart, looked right into my eyes and said, "My mommy gots a new toof-brush!"; I had a dream last night of a lion and a lioness; a call to a friend in Canada was, by chance, right during his fortieth birthday celebration; the weather Tuesday began cold and cloudy with high scudding fog but by noon it was warm and sunny; and we had some old friends that we had not seen for a while over for dinner and they said they were very happy to see us and we had good, animated conversation.

All these are just little moments in my life, a few out of hundreds and thousands, just as in your life. Why notice them? They remind you, they form you, they deepen your soul, they help put things in the right order, they connect you to the world, and they keep you awake. And on top of all that, they bring you immense pleasure.

Health requires this relaxation,
this aimless life.
This life in the present.

HENRY DAVID THOREAU

27

The Gift of Relaxation

This is the gift of achieving physical and mental ease in your body, in your dwelling, in your country, and in the world. It is knowing that you belong and where you belong. Without a minimum amount of true relaxation, we undertake any endeavor from a disadvantaged basis. Humans simply were not made to stay in a state of stress all the time.

Over the centuries, our bodies have changed very little while our culture has changed dramatically. When the hormones that trigger the fight-or-flight response were coursing through the body of the caveman, he was almost always facing a physical stressor: he either killed the woolly mammoth or was killed by it. For us humans now, most stress is not physical but psychological or spiritual. If you get an unfair evaluation at work because of a petty jealousy of your supervisor, what can you do? Fight (which means confronting the supervisor or other authorities, even though you know you'll lose) or flight (which means quitting your job and starting over.)? Generally we can do neither. Both responses are unsatisfactory.

But our bodies were made to do one or the other and the hormones are coursing through our veins on that mission. That negative stress energy has to go somewhere and do something. *It does not go away on its own.* Most often, what it does is attack its host: you. You get sick, irritable, backaches, shoulder aches, flu, colds, fat, or thin; whatever form your stress takes. That is, unless you do something about it.

I believe many people today have seldom known real relaxation and thus all of their projects begin with a handicap. Perhaps they have lived with so much tension and stress from childhood that they are unaware of what they are carrying and it feels normal to them. That's a serious problem. Learning how to relax is crucial to our physical and emotional well-being.

I use the term *relaxation* both in its ordinary sense, what we all mean when we say we feel relaxed, and in a slightly more clinical sense, the return of a person to normal equilibrium, or balance, after a period of stress. In other words, once you have experienced stress in your life, you need to do something with that negative stress-energy in order to balance the time of stress with an opposite time of being relaxed. You can't just return to normal without a relaxation time and expect to have real recovery from the stress. Remember, the negative stress energy does not go away by itself; it accumulates and, if not balanced by a time of relaxation, continues to do you harm. Understanding this is key to true relaxation.

RESPONSE TO STRESS

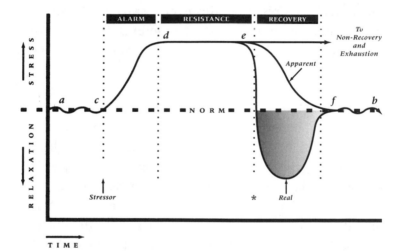

(Based on model of Emmett Miller, M.D.)

Use the diagram on page 135 to picture it graphically: The dotted line begins on the left with point a and ends on the right with point b; this is your normal lifeline. Above the line you are in stress territory and below the line you are in relaxation territory. Your life begins at point a and travels toward point b. A little way along, a stressor occurs (point c), say someone recklessly cuts in front of you in traffic, nearly causing a serious accident and scaring you enough to make your heart pound and your muscles tighten from a rush of adrenaline. That stress event moves you up through the initial alarm-stage (c to d) and above the line well into stress territory. It would be common for one to feel the stress from this event for days or even weeks after. The resistance stage (d to e) is the time you spend actually coping with the stress. It can last from a few moments to years.

Now here's the important point: If you merely return to your normal lifeline at point e and continue on your way, you have not fully recovered from the stress. You still carry the effects of the stress though you might not be aware of it; it accumulates with others that are already there. For real recovery, you must go below the line into relaxation territory for a time and *then* return back up to the line of normal life at point f. Only then are you truly recovered from the stress. For every time above the line (in stress territory) you need a balancing time below the line (in relaxation territory). The times spent in each don't necessarily have to be equal, but you do need time in both territories for real recovery.

Stopping is spending time below the line. Stopping can bring true relaxation to some people for the first time in their lives. This is especially true of people who have lived with long-term stressors like chronic illness (of self or others), abusive relationships, unfair work situations, unavoidable meanness, dysfunctional families or businesses, or social conditions so chaotic and uncontrolled that every moment is a moment of crisis where anxiety is the norm. It is also true for many people who have slipped into workaholism. So many of us are used to living above the line, in stress territory, that we can't even conceive of why we would need to spend time below the line, let alone figure out how to get there!

What does time below the line look like for you? These are your clues for Stopovers. It will be different for everyone and even different at various times of your life. Is it walking, swimming, loafing at your ease, watching trees, or reading poetry? The essential characteristic of time below the line is recovery of balance.

Stillpoints are the good friends of relaxation. Breathing and remembering are natural relaxants: they cause the body's autonomic nervous system to relax and recover. To increase the relaxation factor, add a few stretches, notice where you are holding tension in your body, and then breathe relaxing energy into it.

Unlike achieving things worth having,
to achieve things worth being usually
requires long periods of solitude.

MEYER FRIEDMAN AND RAY ROSENMAN

28

The Gift of Solitude

Being comfortable with aloneness is the gift of solitude.
It also includes the gift of introspection, which is the ability
to look into yourself. Silence is often an attendant benefit.
Pre-millennial life affords most of us very little solitude
and, yet, time alone is essential to a balanced life.

"Solitude is a basic human need. We need to get away
from the noise and from being with other people," says
Anthony Storr, a British psychologist who has written
extensively on solitude.

A lot happens when you are alone. Recall the poet
Rilke's words: "I am the rest between two notes" that are
"reconciled," but only in that "dark interval." What happens in a dark interval is subtle and slow, with gentle

nuances. When you try to imagine a dark interval between two notes in a piece of music, it seems to be a place where you must trust. You have to let go of the note that is now finished, is no longer needed, and, indeed, is now dead. But the new note is not yet there. This is also a place of solitude in which you wonder: Will the new note really come? Will it be what I expect and need right now?

The dark interval is a place of transformation. At this moment of pause, your song has come just so far; when this momentary pause is finished the song will be new, transformed, and perhaps even sent to a new octave or key. But one thing is sure: it will not be the same. After this pause it will be a new and different song.

So solitude transforms. When you come from a time of aloneness, you are a different you. The transformative nature of solitude underscores the overall significance of Stopping. The success of your life depends to a great extent upon the quality of the pauses between the events of your life. The cumulative effect of the pauses determines not only the greatness of the music, but, more important, whether *this* is the song *you* want to be singing.

It is not accidental that the great spiritual leaders of history spent a great deal of time withdrawn, apart, or alone; that is, Stopped.

One of the goals of solitude is to be comfortable with your own company, to get to know and like yourself better, and to appreciate the wonderful work of art you are.

Are you not used to thinking of yourself that way? If not, please try it. Solitude will help. Often the difference between solitude and loneliness is friendship with yourself.

I don't in any way mean to say that those who are not attracted to solitude have low self-esteem. Natural introversion or extroversion are influential too. People who tend to be introverted are naturally more interested in the internal activity of the soul, while extroverts are more attracted to the soul's expressions in the outside world. One is not better than the other; they are just different. Introverts might seek solitude more easily and more often, but we all need it to some degree.

Anthony Storr also says that "the capacity to be alone . . . becomes linked with self-discovery and self-realization and with becoming aware of one's deepest needs, feelings, and impulses." When you are alone, many things can happen that busy-ness and the presence of others disallows: feelings, understandings, remembrances, realizations, priorities, decisions, graces, and so on.

Solitude is the place for introspection: looking into your own soul and discovering there who you are, examining your life, and taking stock. It is the place that allows the internal scanning of Stopping to happen and, thus, is perhaps the most fearful of the seven traits because it allows things to come up. It is also the trait that, when embraced, can bring you previously unknown peace and calm when you discover that what is there isn't as bad as you had feared.

Sue Halpern has also written on solitude. Her lesson in *Migrations to Solitude* was that "the days got longer. The texture of our lives became smoother." She gets to the nature of Stopping when she says, "I had set up this paradigm, in which you either live in solitude—you are completely alone—or you live as the rest of us do. I see that it doesn't work that way. I see now that there are degrees of solitude, and it's more about calmness." Her "degrees of solitude" are the Stillpoints, Stopovers, and Grinding Halts of Stopping.

If being alone is daunting to you, try it in small increments and with an easy way out if you need it. Start with a Stillpoint of just a few moments alone, but with others close by, and build up to a Stopover of a couple of hours on an isolated beach or park. Each increment will increase your comfort, peace, and calm.

A temptation with solitude is to see only isolation from others rather than solitude with self. Doris Grumbach, in *Fifty Days of Solitude,* says "what others regard as a retreat from them or a rejection of them is not those things at all but instead a breeding ground for greater friendship, a culture for deeper involvement, eventually, with them." The purpose of solitude is to improve moments of companionship. Stopping is not at all isolationist—just as the purpose of Stopping is going, so the purpose of solitude is that, when you *are* with people, you are more present and responsive.

I am often asked, "Can you do Stopping with someone

else?" I would rather say that you can do Stopping at the same time as someone else, and probably in the same place, but the nature of Stopping in all three forms is solitary. Whether it is for one minute or one month, it is a coming back to *yourself*, which is by nature an individual act.

Another common question about Stopping is, "Can watching television be Stopping?" For children and young people, definitely not. For adults? Probably not, is my first answer. It's certainly not for me. For some reason, when the TV is on, I cannot *not* attend to it. But I have a friend who can totally space out the TV. It can be blaring and obnoxious, and he really is capable of not hearing it. For people like him, perhaps watching TV can be a low-grade, better-than-nothing, way to Stop.

Writer Sharon Herbstman, discussing the physical and psychological benefits of solitude, says, "watching television and sleeping don't count; the benefits of solitude come from being able to think freely." I agree.

I don't know how to define noise, but I know it when I hear it and I hate it. Noise robs us of attention, relaxation, and solitude. Unfortunately, it is all around us, in the country as well as the city. So one of the dearest results of solitude is silence. For starters, "silence is one of the simplest, most valuable relaxation tools we have," says Edwin Kelley, director of the Insight Meditation Society. On its own, it brings you down below the stress line. Can you identify oases of solitude that are also places of quiet in your part of the world? The cool quiet of an empty church? A museum? The woods near your home?

"Silence is golden," we were told as children by adults who wanted peace and quiet. Now we know what they meant. Silence also comes in a different but no less appreciated form: the absence of words. English novelist George Eliot said, "Blessed is the man who, having nothing to say, abstains from giving us wordy evidence of the fact." In my counseling office, I keep a small, framed reminder to myself: "It often shows fine command of the language to say nothing."

Be by yourself. Be quiet. Just be. These are the gifts of solitude and its attendant silence.

29

The Gift of Openness

Stopping also brings openness, an ability to receive the gifts the world has to offer and to learn the lessons of life because you noticed them. What I most want to communicate by the word *open* is contained in the following words, addressed to a young poet, from the poet Rainer Maria Rilke: "If the angel deigns to come it will be because you have convinced her, not by tears but by your humble resolve to be always beginning: to be a beginner."

To be a beginner is the ultimate of all spiritual endeavors. The beginner knows she has something to learn; the expert "knows" the answers and he is thus cut off from possibilities.

Being open includes being teachable. This can be a challenge for many of us. Teachable is a characteristic that might appear to be a weakness because it can mean "able to be led," but it also means you are capable of recognizing what is appropriate and valuable and pursuing it. It does not mean "being able to be led around by a leash."

Being receptive is also a part of being open. It is the ability to take something or someone into your heart and mind. This is perhaps even more of a challenge. It sounds negative. Our culture tells us—especially men—not to be receptive but to be proactive and aggressive. Receptive is also equated with weakness.

In this way, our attitude toward receptiveness buys into sexism and our fear of the feminine. The feminine is, at least traditionally and stereotypically, receptive. The ideal, of course, is a balance and a complementarity. But there's little doubt that the aggressive wins out for many of us, men or women. It's what is generally rewarded in our culture. The more open and receptive professions—social work, counseling, teaching, or nursing, for example—are at the lower economic end of the scale, which indicates the value society places on such traits.

Why is receptivity necessary? Think of it as the most important way of gaining information, insight, knowledge, or anything. Successful life demands teachability and receptivity from all of us. The most obvious example, perhaps, is the role of student. To be a good student, one must be receptive—or teachable—at least part of the time. To get anything, you must be receptive to it. If we are not comfortable with being receptive, we'll miss much of the point of what comes our way; we just don't see it, even though it may have appeared before our eyes.

Try to conceive it this way: If all you are is action, you never get the feedback you desperately need to understand the result of your action. It is the heart of learning to know what happened as a result of what you did. Then, when you return to your active mode, you will be acting in a way that is based on the information you got by being receptive. You have created a feedback loop of information and power.

In the technique of biofeedback, you are hooked up to sensors that read your body and the level of your stress. As you experiment with ways of inducing relaxation, the machine indicates the decrease or increase in your stress level. Thus you learn to do what works and to avoid what doesn't. The trait of openness is a way of creating your own biofeedback machine. You're open, you notice, and you learn.

Open is a good way to describe the person who is capable of receiving what is available: spontaneous expressions of life, surprises, and new things.

My favorite feast of the liturgical calendar is the feast of the Epiphany. It's celebrated in early January and notes the moment that the Christ child was presented to the Wise Men from the East and, in the fuller sense, shown or manifested to the world. *Epiphania* is the Greek word for appearance or manifestation. I like this feast because it leads to a broader meaning: Epiphanies are all those big or little moments when we realize something, get something for the first time, have a "vision," see something manifested like never before, or achieve a new understanding of how life is and how we fit into it. For those who are open, we can celebrate many epiphanies during the year.

Openness includes the characteristic of being non-self-judgmental. As self-awareness increases with Stopping, it is essential not to jump in and judge what we see in a negative way. Many of us have a harsh inner critic that will immediately say about any of our self-insights, "Oh, that's bad!" The more complete the openness, the more absent, or less severe the judgment.

Effective listening is also the result of developing healthy openness. Instead of thinking of what you are going to say in response as someone speaks to you, you listen—you become receptive—to the other person. You take in consciously what they say, which means you notice their tone of voice, their body language, their vocabulary, and, thus, the real meaning of what they are saying. In this way, your response is much more likely to be appropriate, accurate, and effective.

But before listening to others, you must listen to yourself. Frederick Buechner, a well-known writer and minister, says it so clearly in *Now and Then:* "If I were called upon to state in a few words the essence of everything I was trying to say both as a novelist and as a preacher, it would be something like this: Listen to your life. See it for the fathomless mystery that it is." Stopping is listening to your life so that you become open enough to hear everything there is to hear. Without Stopping, we become so full of the day-to-day that we can't take in the information we need—our glass is full to overflowing and can take in no more. Stopping in all its forms allows the glass (you) to empty and therefore be able to receive even more.

Are you open to becoming more teachable and receptive? Society often neither encourages nor rewards these traits, even though it demands them for advancement. Openness will feel strange and scary if you are not used to it. As an experiment, sit in a chair in a quiet room where you will not be disturbed. Keep your eyes open and relax as much as possible for a period of five minutes while making an attempt to do absolutely nothing, mentally or physically, except to notice your breathing and what happens to you. Be as open and receptive as possible and notice whatever comes to you—thoughts, feelings, or sensations. That's all.

If that sounds daunting, it might be easier for you to just hang out. Plan a few hours with nothing, absolutely nothing, specific on your agenda and just see what happens. Develop your ability to take stock of yourself (What am I feeling now?) and your surroundings (What is going on here?). You will be surprised what, after a time, you will notice. The crucial point is to stay with it precisely when you feel like ending it.

Openness emphasizes listening (not talking), receiving (not giving), being cared for (not taking care of), quiet (not noise), observing (not acting), noticing (not commenting), and learning (not teaching). Notice that the characteristics in parentheses are not negative or in any way bad, they're just not what is needed for Stopping.

Healthy boundaries are flexible enough
that we can choose what to let in
and what to keep out.

ANNE KATHERINE

30

The Gift of Boundaries

Emotional boundaries are a complex psychological subject. The ability to know where you end and the other person begins, to be clear about what is emotionally yours and what is not, and to have people in your life in the places and in the ways that you want them, these are all beneficial for Stopping. Having strong but flexible emotional boundaries is being able to successfully live in community. This gift encourages your involvement with the world, but helps you to avoid unhealthy enmeshment with it.

An easy way to understand this is by thinking of yourself as a house. When the house across the street burns down, you feel bad, but you have not burned down, and you go on about your life. When someone gives the house next to you a new coat of paint you are perhaps happy for that house but you don't brag about it, because it is not your coat of paint.

And as for people (continuing to use a house as a metaphor), there are some you may want outside your gate, some you want in your living room, a few you want in your kitchen, those that you want in the attic, one that you want in your bedroom, and so on. Having good boundaries is having everyone where you want them and not necessarily where they want to be. Now what does this have to do with Stopping?

It's really only with some degree of Stopping, particularly Stopovers and Grinding Halts, that you can find out where everyone is in your house. Stopping is like saying, "OK, everybody out of here for a while and I'll tell you when—and if—you can come back and where I want you!" Maybe you'll find out there is no one at all in your house or even inside your garden gate, and you would like to have some people there. Only when we notice where our boundaries are (or aren't) can we make choices about them.

Longer forms of Stopping, as well as Stillpoints, also help to distinguish another boundary issue: Which are truly your feelings and which are not. Another way of saying this is that Stopping helps you know the difference between yourself and everyone else.

I once observed a family in a park having a picnic lunch: mother, father, and two small children. The parents began to argue. As the parents' argument escalated to the point of yelling at each other, I observed the children's emotional states change to mimic their parents'. The children began pouting, clutching at their parents, whimpering, crying, and eventually screaming. As the parents resolved their difference, the children, too, went back to a state of peaceful picnicking. The children could not distinguish their own feelings from their parents'. That's appropriate for children, but unhealthy for adults. Your pain and joy are not mine, nor is mine yours. We can care about each other—have compassion—without losing our boundaries.

The ability to build community is an important result of healthy boundaries. In *Intimacy and Solitude*, Stephanie Dowrick, speaking of intimacy, says, "Without some acceptance of that 'essential aloneness' which is part of the human condition, the experience of closeness [to others] is often difficult." Her "essential aloneness" is what I call being boundaried. There's a paradox again: by clarifying boundaries, by emphasizing what separates us from one another, we actually have the ability to become closer and, thus, the community is served.

Pablo Neruda has a poem titled "Keeping Quiet." In it he says that if we were really to be quiet we would all experience a "sudden strangeness."

A sudden strangeness. We know that feeling, right? We experience it at various moments of life: in an elevator when all are quiet, doing nothing, and feeling self-conscious in the presence of others; in a subway or on a bus in the silence that follows an angry outburst from a deranged passenger; or in a conversation with friends when one of them suddenly speaks out in unexpected anger or truth. In these moments, we are often anxious to get out and move away to free ourselves of the discomfort and, generally, we do just that. But what if we had to stay and deal with the sudden strangeness? Simply stated: we would then begin to become a community.

Community is people living together and caring for each other. The care is expressed by a willingness to deal with everything that is important to at least one of the members. To do this, boundaries are urgently necessary; otherwise, a state of enmeshment results wherein no one knows who's who and what's whose. Working out how we are to establish and maintain our individual boundaries is how we become a group.

During Stopping, especially the remembering part, self-identity is strengthened and clarified. Remembering where you came from and who you are adds power to your borders so that you don't lose yourself in others and don't allow others to lose themselves in you. When we are together in this way, we can be effective.

*Keep your face to the sunshine
and you cannot see the shadow.*

ATTRIBUTED TO HELEN KELLER

31

The Gift of Embracing Your Shadow

Shadow is a term that comes to us from the psychologist
Carl Jung. He called it an archetype, or a pattern of perception, that we all hold in our consciousness. It refers to that
secret and often fearful part of ourselves that we generally
like to keep hidden and pretend doesn't exist. Jung's
insight was to identify the shadow as a positive force and a
means to self-understanding. A hidden shadow can cause
problems; it's an enemy we don't know. But if we look at
that hidden part of ourselves and learn to embrace it, we
grow in self-understanding and transform an enemy into a
wonderful gift.

The process of Stopping allows time to encounter and
ultimately embrace the shadow. When Stopped, I see things
in myself that I normally ignore. The self-conversations in

my head might go like this: Yes, I see that my shadow is actually a jealous tyrant; I don't like that part of myself but I have to admit, in truth, that it's there; generally my feelings of envy are under control but sometimes they jump out and get me into trouble; or I do and say what I would rather, given my rational preference, not do or say. If I acknowledge that envious self, try to find out what he craves, wants, and needs to tell me, maybe I can turn that energy to good use.

Embracing the shadow is acknowledging that nothing is either black or white, but a portion of both. When we project our shadow out—that is, when I point to you as the one who is causing all the trouble—we deny it in ourselves. The truth is there is no "evil empire," no group or groups, or individuals that are the cause of our suffering and the world's evil. *We all are the causes.* When we deny or avoid our shadow, it not only has its nasty way with us, it can actually cause great harm, even death, to others.

Facing our Shadow during Stopping can be scary. "When one first sees the shadow clearly," says Jungian scholar John A. Sanford, "one is more or less aghast." When I was a boy, my brother and I would listen to *The Shadow* on the radio. The part of the program that I remember vividly is the beginning with the scary music and a man's deep, sinister voice asking, "What evil lurks in the hearts of men? The Shadow knows!" The voice would trail off in menacing and foreboding laughter. It scared us. It still scares people. What indeed *does* my Shadow know? Do I also know it? Will it surprise and scare me? What if I can't handle it? That's where courage comes in.

Alexander Solzhenitsyn, Russian dissident and novelist, said, "If only there were evil people somewhere insidiously committing evil deeds, and it were necessary only to separate them from the rest of us and destroy them. But the line dividing good and evil cuts through the heart of every human being." That includes mine and yours. If we could have the courage to embrace our scary shadows, we would thereby take a giant leap to heal our deep and lasting pain.

Stopping is a process whereby you can—especially if this is scary for you—gradually shake hands with your Shadow. By first specifically acknowledging only your *desire* at some time to embrace your Shadow, you can bring some safety and control to the process by taking it at your own pace.

M. Scott Peck, speaking of evil in *The Road Less Traveled and Beyond*, says, the "central defect of evil is not the sin but the refusal to acknowledge it." The refusal to acknowledge our dark tendencies is the central defect, not the dark tendencies. As Solzhenitsyn said, those tendencies are always with us; both good and evil are in *all* our hearts. Only when I can acknowledge *all* parts of me, can I move from childhood to maturity, from isolation to community, and from running and covering to peace and equanimity.

Sometimes the fear of the Shadow takes the form of truly believing that you are so busy you can't stop. At a successful, midsized business with a staff of about sixteen people, the owner noticed one of her employees becoming more and more stressed but never taking time off, not even her earned vacation time, yet always saying how overworked she was. "I specifically tried to give her permission and enthusiastic encouragement to take time off. 'Take the afternoon off, Faith,' I would say to her, but always she answered, 'I can't. I have too much to do.' Even when I said, 'It's okay if you don't get it all done, you need to relax and get away from here,' it was the same response. 'No, I can't.'" I see this as evidence that the hidden and unembraced Shadow has much power and many of us will do anything we can to avoid looking at it.

It is also a trickster. It can make a lie look like the truth, a fiction like a fact, and a doubt like a conviction. Because it's a trickster, it can take many forms, even the form of innocence.

The gift of acknowledging your shadow is the antidote to the often dangerous oversimplification of the innocent Pollyanna. During the time of training for my counseling degree, I had the opportunity to take a class from Daniel Berrigan, S.J., the renowned Jesuit peace activist, author, and teacher. He spoke to us eloquently about "terrible innocence." Terrible innocence is an attitude which, while looking into the face of evil, it prompts us to deny it, avoid it, pretend not to notice it, or feign ignorance while, in our hearts, we really know what's going on. It brings the false innocence of sweetness and light to a moment of possibly serious harm. That indeed is terrible innocence; terrible because it allows me to stand idle in the presence of evil. That's also a well-hidden Shadow.

That's what Stopping can help us to uncover and heal.

*A calling may be postponed, avoided, intermittently
missed . . . but eventually it will out.*

JAMES HILLMAN

32

The Gift of Purpose

Purpose is the wonderful gift of Stopping that encourages us to go out from ourselves, to listen to what we
might hear from the universe, and to discover our unique
role in life. Purpose means that someone or something
outside of you is looking at you and calling your name;
you are being called to accomplish an objective, to be
someone that only you can be, and to realize what is most
essentially you. Another word to express the same idea is
calling. The idea of vocation serves well. Stopping helps
you to clarify or even discover your purpose, to hear your
calling, and to realize your vocation.

Purpose is knowing that there is something far beyond
us. And knowing that means that there are lots of events,

moments, and realities of life that are not immediately identifiable and explainable by just the facts that we can see and prove. The sense of having a purpose gives balance to our human situation: not only do we meet the divine as we look within ourselves, as surely we do, but in the same moments of Stopping, we meet the divine in the call that reaches to us from beyond ourselves. This beyondness is the distinctive characteristic that underscores the importance of this gift of Stopping.

Having purpose acknowledges that you are named to be something that only you can be. Your challenge is to find it, discover it, wrestle with it, or do whatever is necessary to realize it.

James Hillman, an ever-insightful, if controversial, author, writes about this idea from a somewhat different perspective in his book, *The Soul's Code*. His theory, the acorn theory, briefly stated, is that we are born with a calling and the object of all of life is to discover and realize that calling. Hillman calls this *growing down* into the acorn. Instead of looking ahead to what we might become as we try to realize our inner potential, he suggests that we look back at the call we had been given at birth, even before birth, and try to allow its fulfillment. Realizing one's calling is to look out to the world for signs as well as back to the seed or gift with which we were born.

I believe he's on to something. If we miss this element of our Stopping experiences or if we only concentrate on validating our very personal desires and yearnings, we run a real risk of seeing the world purely subjectively and from a narrow point of view and, thus, of becoming selfish, overbearing, patronizing, and self-righteous. It can also make it easy to get stuck blaming someone else for our problems and to take ourselves way too seriously.

Trying to identify, to clarify, and to respond to our purpose, or trying to hear and realize our call, takes our gaze out to the world's horizons and up to God to see what in the world or what in the heavens is calling on us for service, for help, for joy, for entertainment, or for whatever it is that only we can give. And it also takes our gaze back into our personal histories to search for clues. It frees us from allowing introspection to become overly impressed with subjective intuitions and gives the objective intuitions a chance.

Purpose and calling have a power of their own; they always want to come out and have life. Having a sense of your calling is having a sense of the presence of something other than yourself. Perhaps when you were younger there was a moment when you came in touch with that something beyond. You knew that you wanted to do something and to be something. Perhaps it just struck you and you knew or maybe it was more subtle. As Hillman says, "The call may have been more like gentle pushings in the stream in which you drifted unknowingly to a particular spot on the bank." As you look back, you have a sense that something beyond you was involved. It is also important to remember that it is never too late to hear your call; now is *always* the right time.

Hillman tells a story about world famous singer Ella Fitzgerald. As a young girl she was in an amateur night event. She was introduced: "Miss Fitzgerald here is gonna dance for us . . . Hold it, hold it. Now what's your problem, honey? . . . Correction, folks. Miss Fitzgerald has changed her mind. She's not gonna dance, she's gonna sing." She won first prize. Though she had meant to dance, something told her to sing, and that was the start of a long, successful career. Hillman tells the story to demonstrate his acorn theory and that it often shows itself early and unexpectedly.

The gift of purpose is especially realized during the longer times of Stopovers and Grinding Halts, dealing as they do with the broad questions of calling and vocation.

It isn't only the famous of the world who have a purpose. We all do. And most often it does not make itself known as dramatically or as early as Ella Fitzgerald's. Stopping is very much about recognizing and realizing your calling and identifying and fulfilling your purpose. We have to be still, quiet, undistracted, and awake enough to hear it. For to miss it would be tragic.

IV

Exploring
the Challenges
of
Stopping

There is more to life than
increasing its speed.

Mohandas Gandhi

33

Moving Down to the Roots

We are at a critical point on our journey with Stopping because we now have enough information to see that Stopping asks us to do something radical. Stopping is not complicated, is not difficult to understand, and is not even difficult to do. But it is radical. Stopping is not slowing down. Stopping is stopping. The effect will be to slow us down, yes, but the primary act is doing nothing, ceasing activity, and being still.

"Radical?" you might think, "I don't do radical!" But radical can be very simple. Banish the common images associated with it—starvation fasts, street riots, or someone's liberation army—and simply move the energy down deep and into your roots.

That's what radical really means. Here's Webster's definition of radical: "from a root or relating to the origin: fundamental." Stopping brings you to your origins and to what is fundamentally you. It brings you to your true home. It reaches deeply into your soul. And we don't go there often; we're not used to the territory because the problem of too much is keeping us distracted.

Take a moment and allow yourself to form a mental image of a tree. What you probably have in your mind's eye is really only part of a tree: the part you see. But the whole tree includes a root structure as broad and deep as the branches are high and wide. A whole tree is actually a trunk between two equal masses of branches and roots.

Stopping is an energy that is radical because it takes you down to the roots of the tree that is you, down to the sources of your life. Those roots, which are not so obvious but are essential, are the necessary balance to the more active, external, and obvious branches of life.

So if Stopping is so great and wonderful, is so easy to do, and gives so many benefits, why don't we all just do it? Because we have received powerful anti-Stopping messages from society telling us it is bad, and because most of us are afraid of what we'll discover down there in the roots of ourselves; we're unfamiliar with the territory and we want to avoid it, if possible.

The goal of this section is to help you feel competent and confident as you deal with the challenges you may encounter with Stopping. To that end, please keep these important facts in mind: the fears you might face as you are Stopped are almost always not as bad as you might think; there are ways to deal with them that are satisfying and effective; if you have some overwhelming fears, there are safe ways to get help; and to not face your fears is to leave unexplored way too much of a vibrant, gift-filled life.

Our first challenge is the intense and potent anti-Stopping messages our culture has been imparting to us since childhood.

*We have lived not in proportion to the
number of years we have spent on the earth,
but in proportion as we have enjoyed.*

Henry David Thoreau

34

When Society Says "Don't"

We live in a world that is not very open or friendly to
Stopping. Our society's voices often say, "Keep going,
don't stop!" So in order to Stop, we need to release the
hold that our culture's unspoken but powerful messages
have on us. Here are some of the ideas behind the anti-
Stopping voices:

- Leisure is a luxury you can't afford.

- Pleasure-seekers end up in hell.

- To get ahead you must work more hours.

- You have to keep up with the Joneses.

- Doing nothing is slothful and lazy.

- If it's faster, it's obviously better.

- Growth is always good.

- Money is always the bottom line.

- More is always better than less.

- Play is only for children.

The list of lies is endless, and it is often very difficult to resist believing them. They sound pretty good. We often hear them coming from our own lips.

When we stop to think about them, we know that these statements are not true. But *only* when we Stop to think about them. If we don't, the danger is that they will have their way with us. We get distracted, we forget, and it's easier to just go along with them. Notice that they all argue against Stopping and taking time out for yourself and for those around you.

There are also many voices saying that, in effect, life is a most serious business. But just what does *serious* mean? The dictionary indicates that its first and most important meaning is "thoughtful." So in that case, yes, life must be serious and we must live it thoughtfully. But not grimly. The word *serious* with its meanings of "grim, heavy, no-fun-allowed, and painful," I would suggest, is not applicable to Stopping.

Often, it seems, organized religions can give the idea

that life is serious in the grim kind of way. One need only think of the imperiousness of Vatican pronouncements, of the Seven Deadly Sins, and of the rules, regulations, and prohibitions of many religions. The international memorial of the Protestant Reformation in Geneva, Switzerland, supports this as well. The memorial is a three-hundred-foot-long wall of granite with fifteen-foot statues of an unsmiling Calvin, Knox, and Cromwell who are protected by an equally long moat of water; it says serious with a capital *S*. And the depictions of Moses with the Ten Commandments? Nothing to be taken lightly for sure.

I want to be the first to support religions in their effort to make us more thoughtful about how we live our lives. I also want to be the first to speak against their unfortunate propensity to kill people's spirits by oppressive, grim, and meaningless injunctions and attitudes. Life is hard enough on its own. Let's not needlessly multiply sins. We have enough of those, too.

Robert Ornstein and David Sobel understand this idea and express it in their book, *Healthy Pleasures.* They say, "Combining an archaic religiosity with a sensory-deprived world is to place two prisons together. The result is a life lost not only to this world but to the next." *Archaic religiosity* is a false or excessive religiousness. Combine that with our tendency to ignore the pleasures of the natural world and, say the authors, you are succeeding not only in missing life on earth, but are also trying to bully your way into a very restrictive heaven with a frowning and determined grimace on your face. Who would want to go to *that* kind of heaven?

I learned a lesson about this from my mother. I was a newly ordained priest and trying very hard to get it all right, which got twisted into taking myself too seriously. After mass one morning, while on a visit home, my mother introduced me to two small children who were clearly afraid of me as I went to shake their hands. They pulled away and held on to their mother. It was politely overlooked by everyone, but later my mother said to me in her quiet way, "Perhaps you were acting a bit severe." I clearly remember her word: *severe*. This was my gentle mother's understated way of saying, "Lighten up, you're not all *that* important!" Had I been Stopped enough to have recognized my own overseriousness and been able to lighten up, the children would have sensed it immediately and there could have been a soulful connection rather than a distancing space.

Stopping is time spent with ourselves, especially the longer times of Stopovers and Grinding Halts, that we all need in order to keep our perspective and not take ourselves too seriously.

Writer Mark Matousek tells of a wonderful moment in his life that demonstrates this idea. For half an hour he was trying to explain his spirituality to his friend, expounding on all the intricacies of self and no-self, on liberation and enlightenment, and on the teachings of inspiring gurus and saints. When he was finished, his friend, after a long pause, smiled and asked, "Do you mean kindness?"

G. K. Chesterton, British novelist and poet, captures this

idea wonderfully: "The reason angels can fly is that they take themselves so lightly."

Stopping says "No!" to the voices that say "It's selfish to take time for yourself"; "Life is by its very nature a grimly serious affair"; and "Laugh at others' foibles but not at your own." In this way, Stopping is countercultural. It is not afraid to say "No" and say it strongly. It encourages you to discover your own voice, your own priorities, your own wisdom, and your own fun.

The problems we have with Stopping are generally not intellectual problems. Often we know exactly what is good for us and what, given our best moment, we would choose. Our problem is the one St. Paul groused about in his letter to the community in Rome: "Those things I wish to do, I do not; those I wish to avoid, those I do" (Rom. 7:17–19). Stopping is a way to assure that the things you want are the things you actually do.

Speaking of St. Paul, here's another opportunity to remember to be patient with yourself as you go about incorporating Stopping into your life. Paul was so hurried, driven, and work-oriented that he had to be Stopped. He was literally knocked off his horse to the ground and made blind so that he had to spend Stopover-time in Damascus doing nothing, in order to become more fully awake and remember who he was. Sound familiar? When he did awaken and remember, his vision returned and he changed the world.

I've lived! I've got to find out what to do now!

AGNES GOOCH IN *Auntie Mame*

35

"I'm Afraid!"

"I am afraid of the whole world," said poet Pablo Neruda. "Fear of life is the favorite disease of the twentieth century," said writer William Lyon Phelps. So as we move our energy and our focus down to our roots, the first feeling we are likely to experience is fear.

I wonder if you know that wonderful scene from the movie *Auntie Mame* in which the comical and trouble-prone Agnes Gooch, played by Peggy Cass, painfully pregnant and bewildered, bumbles up the stairs in search of Auntie Mame and says in all her innocent confusion, "Well I've lived! I've got to find out what to do now!?" Her question rises out of the place of fear that we all carry with us at our roots.

If there is any idea that is common to all systems of wisdom, religion, and philosophy, it is the truth that the greatest challenge of one's life is oneself. Fear? Of course. Again the poet sees what we all need to see. In this case, let's look at what Pablo Neruda sees. Read the following poem aloud, if your situation allows; reading it aloud will tend to slow it down and bring it home to you.

Fear
by Pablo Neruda

Everyone is after me to exercise,
get in shape, play football,
rush about, even go swimming and flying.
Fair enough.

Everyone is after me to take it easy.
They all make doctor's appointments for me,
eyeing me in that quizzical way.
What is it?

Everyone is after me to take a trip,
to come in, to leave, not to travel,
to die and, alternatively, not to die.
It doesn't matter.

Everyone is spotting oddnesses
in my innards, suddenly shocked
by radio-awful diagrams.
I don't agree with them.

Everyone is picking at my poetry
with their relentless knives and forks,
trying, no doubt, to find a fly.
I am afraid.

I am afraid of the whole world,
afraid of cold water, afraid of death.
I am as all mortals are,
unable to be patient.

And so, in these brief, passing days,
I shall put them out of my mind.
I shall open up and imprison myself
with my most treacherous enemy,
Pablo Neruda.

What does Neruda tell us about fear? Here's how the poem gets into my head: Everyone is trying to give me advice. Do this, do that! Don't do this, don't do that! I know I'm sick, but I'm still here and I'm still in charge! So I will ignore all of you and do what is most important at a time like this: face my fears and face what has always been my most serious challenge—me.

Between the lines (Remember the spaces between the notes? It's where the most interesting things happen.) I picture Neruda with his wise old face, leaning close to us and whispering into our ears: "I am writing this for you, the one who's reading it. Do it now. Spend time with yourself now, while you still can."

This part of the book takes Neruda's words to heart and Agnes Gooch's question seriously. We will lock ourselves up with our most double-crossing enemies, us, and we will answer Agnes's question, "Now what!?" Let's form the question like this: "Now that I am Stopped, even for a moment, how do I assure myself that I will be okay and that I will not have to face more than I can deal with?

Stopping will feel safe when fears no longer have their way with you. The fears will not necessarily be gone but they will not be in control. And it is, paradoxically, by moving into your fears that you will move out of them.

That paradox is the goal here, to move out of our fears by first moving into them. Moving into them involves three simple processes: noticing, naming, and narrating. Your fears will gradually diminish and lose their power over you as you learn these three processes. First notice, or note, your fears and take them into account; then name your fears; and then narrate, or tell your story of these fears to someone else.

Recall the story of Naaman. He was the general who was hesitant to cure his illness by following the prophet's advice to wash seven times in the river because it seemed too simple and silly to him. Now is a good time to recall the lesson of the story: to respect the power of simple acts. Please don't underestimate the power of these simple acts of the soul: noticing, naming, and narrating.

Silent, hidden enemies are more to be feared
than those that are openly expressed.

CICERO, 106–43, B.C.E.

36

Seeing the Enemy

What's the first thing you notice as you are practicing Stopping? Well, if you are like me, what you'll notice is that your body might be Stopped but your mind goes racing on. And does it race! Sometimes it seems that my mind has a mind of its own. The internal chatter seems endless.

Currently there is a clever advertising creation on television that tries to sell us batteries. It's a mechanical bunny that never stops marching, but just keeps going and going and going . . . and banging its drum, implying, of course, that its batteries are long-lasting.

This advertising animal is an apt metaphor for all the internal chatter, the "tapes" that don't stop playing in your head, and the noise in your mind. Like the bunny, your noisy self-talk just keeps on going, whether you are aware of it or not, whether you are listening or not, and even whether you seem to care or not. And, like the bunny, the chatter goes on willy-nilly, without apparent course, without care for what it's bumping into, and seemingly without end. This tireless bunny is very much a clown. It's purpose almost always is to act as a cover, that is, something that distracts you so that you won't attend to something else— like facing your fears.

So notice it. Just notice it. From this moment on, from time to time, and whenever it occurs to you, notice what your internal chatter is saying.

By noticing it, you will gain just a bit of control over it and maybe even quiet it down occasionally. Quieting the noise of internal chatter is a goal of Stopping and—understanding this was a breakthrough for me—this is a goal no one can ever fully accomplish. It is a challenging task, a part of what Jack Kornfield in *A Path with Heart,* calls "stopping the war" we carry within us. Saints, monks, and spiritual masters all tell us that they are still working on it, so we have to be easy on ourselves. Even if we still it, the chatter will come back. That's the nature of being human.

Here are some questions for your internal noise: Is your chatter in the form of actual words and sentences? Does it have the real voice of someone you know? Maybe a parent, a boss, or a friend? Does it happen more on certain occasions than on others? Is your chatter more like pictures or movie scenes that keep running through your head? Maybe your chatter takes the form of "worry cycles," which are, as Herbert Benson describes in *Beyond the Relaxation Response*, "unproductive . . . circuits that cause the mind to 'play' over and over . . . the same . . . uncreative, health-impairing thoughts." What is the content of your chatter? Work, family, relationship, or trivia? Just notice it and, please, notice it without judgment.

Noticing means that you do not place a value judgment on yourself for whatever you are noticing. And this is true for all of your Stopping experiences. Whatever comes up, the first thing to do is just let it come up and let it be. That's noticing. I am often tempted to allow judgment to jump right in and ruin it all. The judgment of *I shouldn't be having all that internal noise* is about as appropriate as *I shouldn't have brown eyes*. The noise is just there, that's all. And it's morally neutral; no guilt and no virtue are involved. For those who have been raised in highly structured religious systems, not judging ourselves for experiences and feelings that come on their own can be a challenge.

My own internal chatter is often musical. It can drive me crazy. It happens most often when I am alone, especially when I am walking, which I love to do and do often. I am out, walking briskly, wanting to let go the cares of work and the rest of the day's affairs, and enjoying the physical world. Then the damn music starts. It's in my head, it's not restful, and I find it very difficult to stop. The music can be anything: maybe some piece I just heard on the radio; maybe—I really hate this—an advertising slogan;

or maybe a theme from Beethoven's Sixth. Anything.

What the masters tell me is: "Just notice it, David. That's all. Just notice it." Noticing it is valuable. Noticing it is effective. Noticing it is more powerful than it might at first appear. By noticing your internal chatter, you are weakening its need to exist and letting it know that it's not as powerful as it thinks. As Dawn Groves puts it, in *Meditation for Busy People*, "Simply observe the waterfall of thought." Any enemy—in this case the negative chatter that is working against us—that has been spotted is in a much weaker position than when it had the power of being hidden or unnoticed. Now, ambush is not possible.

What you'll no doubt notice about noticing is that it is also a way of creating a Stillpoint. Add a basic breath or two and focus on the nature of your chatter. This can be a way you do most of your Stillpoints as you bring Stopping into your daily life.

As your internal chatter calms down a bit, what might possibly become more clear are your fears, because those are what the clown of internal chatter is trying to cover and to keep you from noticing so they can continue to have their way with you.

So the next thing is to notice your fears. Just notice them. That's all. Noticing is the opposite of repression or pushing away fears. Instead, it is turning and acknowledging them: Oh, yes, I am afraid of people who talk loudly, I am afraid of heights, of dogs, of dark, and isolated places . . .

I want to say this about fears: don't be surprised if there are none! In my experience with people in therapy, that happens a lot. The fears they expected to find when they turned and faced themselves simply were not there. They can truthfully say, along with Henry David Thoreau, "Nothing is so much to be feared as fear." Eighty years later FDR would say the same thing in his first inaugural address: "We have nothing to fear but fear itself."

"I thought that all these monsters would jump out at me from my deep, dark psychic pool," said my client Roger as he was exploring why his relationships didn't seem to work out as he hoped. In Roger's case, the realization that there were no horrible monsters hiding in wait for him gave him a great deal of confidence, which indeed changed his way of relating to people. It's not that he didn't have any fears at all—we're all afraid of something—but that the fears that were there were not uncontrollable monsters, but just garden-variety fears that he could handle.

Some clients will casually mention a secret and fearful part of their current or past life with the idea, often unspoken, of seeing how I react and to test to see if this is something they should really be afraid of. When I nod in understanding or say something like, "Yes, many people have those kinds of experiences," you can almost detect an audible sigh of relief as the possibly serious fear becomes a manageable part of their life.

But let's say that you indeed find some fears. What would noticing them look like? How would one go about noticing fears? If you were to eavesdrop on my mind as I considered my fears before leaving the priesthood, you would have heard something like this: I am afraid of losing the values that have supported my entire life up to this point; Am I losing my faith?; I fear breaking my solemn, public vows; What will my family and colleagues think of me?; I fear being a failure and being called a failed priest; I am afraid that I will not be able to support myself since this is all I am trained to do; Will I meet someone with whom I will be able to build a lifelong relationship?; Is that even what I want to do?; and, I feel very "out of it" in this area, and dating scares me to death. Believe me the list could go on. I could have said as Neruda said, "I am afraid. I am afraid of the whole world."

During my month-long Grinding Halt, I was able to notice my fears. I just let them come and noted their presence. I logged them, saying, "there's one," "there's another," and "here's another one too." They just came on their own because I was not covering them. I knew they were there, and they "knew" I knew.

Noticing is like being open: you simply take in the information, and mark the presence of, be aware of, note, and store the data. I know you will find that noticing will be more powerful for you than you expected.

HOBBES: *When you're confronted with the stillness of nature, you can even hear yourself think.*

CALVIN: *This is making me nervous. Let's go in.*

BILL WATTERSON, *Calvin and Hobbes*

37

Owning Your Fear

Step two is to name your fears. By naming, I mean any process by which you talk to or talk about your internal chatter and hidden fears. Naming can include actually giving fear a name ("Your name is 'Fear Of Failure!'"), talking to your internal chatter in order to calm it down ("Will you be quiet, please!"), or changing the words you use to talk about them (instead of "I have a terrible temper and it scares me" say, "How do I want to focus this immense power?"). Naming often involves personifying the feelings as if they were individuals, making them "persons" in order to interact with them. That automatically happens when you talk to them: "Hello, Fear of Disapproval, here you are again"; "Oh, here's Fear of Being a Bad Leader, she's an old friend"; "Oh no, it's you, Fear of the Worst Thing Happening, I thought you were gone for good!"

Naming is important because it gives you power over the thing named. Just as when you name a pet or a boat or—especially—your own child, you thus assume a position of power and responsibility over it, so with naming internal noises and fears.

By naming you also are accepting ownership. In effect, you are saying, "These are *my* internal noises. I acknowledge and accept that they are *my* fears and no one else's." Think of it: if they belong to you, as indeed they do, then you can have power over them.

Noises named and fears addressed are noises and fears weakened. Now, you have *them*; they don't have *you*.

Here's one way I use naming: My internal, unasked-for, running commentary—or unrequested musical interlude—often has the effect of making me mad. I get tired of it and exasperated. Actually, there are times when I feel like clobbering that running bunny, both the one on TV and the one in my head. So when I begin to feel that way, I stop, breathe, and notice—a Stillpoint. I continue to notice. Then I do the naming. For example, I'll talk to my internal chatter and music. What I most often say comes from my father.

When I was a boy, playing noisily with a friend up in my room, my father would sometimes yell out from downstairs, "Pipe down up there!" It was effective because he didn't do it often, so it got my attention. As if caught in a freeze-frame, I stopped making noise right then. So now I borrow my father's words. I say, "Pipe down up there!" to my endless chatter and to my unwanted music. Occasionally it helps. Other times I just decide to continue to notice it and maybe try it again later.

So using a phrase or a word—especially one that has meaning to you—can help. By focusing on it and repeating it quietly to yourself, you might quiet the noise. If it doesn't work, just take note of it. Noticing and naming have the effect of weakening those invasive guests.

An effective way to use naming during your Stopping, even during the briefer times, is to name the fears that you hold in your body. Often the body remembers what the mind forgets; it can hold on to fears and make them present to you by pain, tension, aches, stiffness, and soreness. So when you experience an unusual discomfort in your stomach, you might ask, "I wonder what was wrong with that tuna sandwich I had for lunch?" More accurate questions would be, "Who did I have lunch with?" or "What were we talking about?" When your neck and shoulder tension become severe, maybe it's not just the lack of exercise, but the fear you are carrying there. Thus identified, the fear is weakened. By naming, you are asking the right questions.

Carolyn Myss, a medical intuitive, had this insight during a recent interview: "One of the ways I tell people to deal with fear . . . is to change their vocabulary. Start there and the rest will take care of itself. That's how powerful language is." Perhaps your fears are based on always being a victim of life and its situations and always being made to suffer. "If I decide that I am not going to think about myself as a victim anymore," says Myss, "I won't use victim vocabulary. That alone will change my whole life. Once I stop using victim words, I become mindful. It will change your perception and drop it down to your heart, to your feelings, to your self-esteem. It will eventually make the full journey to ground zero."

This is like a self-fulfilling prophesy. If, in referring to myself, even internally, I persist in using vocabulary such as "afraid of being an addictive personality," "afraid of never being able to pick the right partner," or "always needing approval of others," then it's likely that I will persist in those fears. Myss's insight is that changing the words we use to describe our fears is a big step in ridding ourselves of them.

There is one fear that must be named here; it's the fear that is almost always a part of every other fear, especially those that might come to us while we are Stopped. Its name is Fear of Death. Even more powerfully and importantly its name is Fear of My Death. Recall Neruda's poem, "Fear." Another between-the-lines message of the poem is that he realizes he is probably dying and that's really what brings up his fear. Recall also what he does with that fear: he spends time with it and embraces it.

Religious faiths are rich with ways to comprehend, embrace, and give meaning to death. For a contemporary treatment of our cultural tendency to avoid the topic of death, you might read Ernest Becker's *The Denial of Death*. For deepening a compassionate understanding of death, look at Stephen Levine's *Who Dies?*

Here I want only to give it a name: "You are Fear of My Own Death." In naming it I hope to encourage you to acknowledge its presence and to become, if you are not already, comfortable and familiar with it. That we are all in the process of dying need not be sad or depressing. Indeed, embracing that reality can become wonderfully liberating. Our principle still—maybe especially—holds true here: By moving into our fears we move out of them.

I wonder how all those who do not write,
compose, or paint can manage to escape
the . . . fear which is inherent
in the human situation.

GRAHAM GREENE

38

A Telling Relief

Perhaps the most important and most effective thing to do with our fears is to share them with another person. That's what I mean by narrating: telling someone your fears. Telling brings relief. And the more secret and hidden the fear, the more effective and relieving the telling. In fact, this is one way to look at the process of psychotherapy: one person telling, trusting, and sharing their life with another.

For me, one of the most powerful moments in the contemporary literature of psychotherapy is a chapter from Irving Yalom's book, *Love's Executioner*. He tells of a client, an older woman who needed to learn to trust again. Eventually, during the course of one of their counseling sessions, she simply emptied the contents of her purse and told him stories—meanings, values, feelings—about all of the items she carried there and was now taking out, one by one, to show him. It was utterly simple and utterly profound, and she left the session more able to trust, less burdened, less fearful. And he, the therapist, said, "I think it was the best hour of therapy I ever gave."

I remember learning the power of sharing fear from my older sister. I was about eight years old and just beginning to hear and use the forbidden (sinful, dirty, or blasphemous) language of adults and feeling a lot of guilty fear about it. One summer evening, my older sister casually asked me if I had ever said something awful like "God damn it!" I can still feel the blush on my childish Catholic face as I heard the question and felt the guilt. For some reason—probably I could read her goodwill and feel that this was safe—I said, "Yes." I clearly remember her response, "Oh, that's all right, don't worry about it, sometimes I do, too." It was one of those moments of surprise and affirmation. By sharing my guilty fear, I lost it. I thought, "My sister is perfect, and if she did it, it couldn't be too bad," and so, "I am just like everyone else." What relief and acceptance I felt.

To whom can you tell your fears? This is often not an easy question. The answers can be different for everyone. Is it a spouse or partner? Often, they are the most difficult to confide in, either because they are involved in the fear and feel it too closely also or they are too threatened to be able to understand. A parent or sibling? A fortunate number of us have developed such a relationship with a member of the immediate family. Often, though, it will be a friend. A friend with whom you can talk about who you really are. What a gift! A gift to treasure if you have it; one to cultivate if you don't.

Before you share your fear with another, it is like you are alone in your home and hear someone rattling the front door. Your friend's reassurance is a familiar voice outside the door: "Don't be afraid. It's just me." What a comforting announcement; fear is immediately transformed into connection. You are no longer alone with your fears. Or think of the relief of confession. How much better you feel when you have told someone of the burden you carry. The weight is lifted, and the fear is dissipated.

Fear can never completely leave us. In a way, it's necessary. We would not be safe without it. "Early and provident fear is the mother of safety," wrote Edmund Burke, the eighteenth-century Irish author and statesman. Fear helps us to be careful. You would not want to lose completely, for example, a fear of height, of dangerous substances, of aggressive people, or of snarling animals. To do so would be to endanger yourself. No, the fears we are speaking of here are the irrational, the unsubstantiated, the inhibiting, and the self-damaging.

Some of the most wonderful years of my priesthood were spent on my three-and-a-half-year assignment to parish work in Cali, Colombia, South America. Some companions and I had a scary experience there. We got stoned.

No, it's not what you might be thinking. This was well before the time of the Cali cartel. By stoned, I mean literally. Four of us, the religious staff of our parish, a fellow-priest, two Benedictine nuns, and I, were driving to the airport to meet a new member of our team, another Benedictine sister. There had been a recent boycott of all the public busses due to a drastic increase in bus fares. The people simply stopped using the busses, the busses quit running, and the city was paralyzed. Outbreaks of violence were reported; often private automibiles were attacked. But all that was over; it was safe to go out now—or so we thought.

We were in the riot before we knew it. And that we got out of it unharmed still amazes me. We had to drive through mobs of people with stones, many of them rock-sized, as if through a tunnel of terror. The car was hit more than a hundred times—we later counted the dents—the windows were all smashed and we were totally shaken. When it was over, we began to tell each other and anyone who would listen about our experience. We still remind each other of it when we meet to this day. It has, for all of us, been in the telling that we have recovered, that we have learned from it, and that we have tried to place the experience within the context of our lives and, at that time, within the context of our ministry. Imagine trying to keep quiet about such an experience! Even at this moment as I write about it, and thus tell it again, I find new meanings and new lessons, and I remember many more.

Fear can be told in many ways, not just to another individual, but to the world. Throughout human history fears have been the motive of great artistic and scientific expression. As novelist Graham Greene reminds us in the epigraph that opens this chapter, fear motivates artists to speak to the world about their most profound insights. Is this a way for you to narrate your fear? What can your fear lead you to express artistically to all of us who would welcome your perceptions?

The most terrifying thing is to accept oneself completely.

Carl Jung

39

The Doctor's Unthinkable Thought

In the autobiographical *Memories, Dreams, Reflections,* Carl Jung, one of the most eminent physicians and psychologists of the twentieth century, tells a story from when he was about twelve years old. It's a story about overcoming fear by moving into it and noticing, naming, and narrating:

"One fine summer day . . . I came out of school at noon and went to the cathedral square. The sky was gloriously blue, the day one of radiant sunshine. The roof of the cathedral glittered, the sun sparkling from the new, brightly glazed tiles.

"I was overwhelmed by the beauty of the sight, and thought: 'The world is beautiful and the church is beautiful, and God made all this and sits above it far away in the blue sky on a golden throne and . . .' here came a great hole in my thoughts, and a choking sensation. I felt numbed and knew only: 'Don't go on thinking now! Something terrible is coming, something I do not want to think, something I dare not even approach . . . because it would be committing the most frightful of sins.'"

Jung, the pious son of a clergyman, then describes how he did all he could do to keep the vision away and not give into it, how his mother worried about his odd behavior, how he lost sleep, and how he was deeply fearful that if he let the thought come he would plunge himself directly into hell. This was truly a terrified boy.

After going though much mental anxiety, utterly alone in his painful anguish, he finally was able to resolve his conflict: "God also desires me to show courage. And if that is so . . . he will give me his grace. . . . I gathered all my courage, as though I were about to leap forthwith into hellfire, and let the thought come.

"I saw before me the cathedral, the blue sky. God sits on His golden throne, high above the world—and from under the throne an enormous turd falls upon the sparkling new roof, shatters it, and breaks the walls of the cathedral asunder. So that was it! I felt an enormous and indescribable relief."

Clearly, there is much that could be said about the meaning of this earthy and dramatic image. But what is significant for us is that he overcame his fear by moving into it and by letting it come. He says, "Why did God befoul His cathedral? That, for me, was a terrible thought." But it was also an important thought for him, a key element in developing his teaching on the Shadow archetype that is pivotal to the way many understand human nature.

This story from Jung demonstrates so clearly the three processes of dealing with the challenges of Stopping. The noticing: "Something terrible is coming. . . . Something I do not want to think." The naming: "So that was it!"

The narrating takes a little different twist and reminds us that we are not alone in the challenge of telling our fears to others. Says Jung of his experience at the time it occurred: "It would never have occurred to me to speak of my experience openly. . . . I could never have talked about [it] with friends." He indicates that he finally talked about his experience with his wife, but that was many years later. The final narration, of course, was to include it in his memoir. It took him a long time, but finally he told about it.

Lord! teach me the art of taking minute vacations . . .
that I may know . . . there is more to life
than measuring its speed.

ANONYMOUS AMERICAN PRAYER

40

Saying It to God

Prayer can help us find the courage to deal with our fears. I remember a conversation I had with a woman years ago when I was a priest. She was ill and scared of what her illness might bring. I was visiting her at home and we were talking of her illness when she somewhat abruptly changed the topic and said, "Father, I have been concerned for quite a while because I don't seem to pray very well." We chatted about this for a moment and then I asked her, "How do you pray?" With a rather embarrassed look on her face she said, "Well, God and I, we just sit and look at each other. That's all I seem to want to do."

I remember the conversation because that's when I learned a late lesson about prayer and an early lesson about Stopping. That woman was contemplative, even though she would never have used the word to describe herself. She had come to the prayer of quiet. She told God all her fears by merely (merely?) being open to God's presence. Praying can be just hanging out with God. That can lessen fears.

As I am writing this, there have been a spate of articles and studies, some from medically scientific sources, that say that patients who pray, or have doctors who pray with or for them, get better quicker and more completely. Dr. Herbert Benson has presented research that indicates that an ability to combine a simple method of meditation with one's "personal belief system can produce . . . powerful inner effects." What scientists have discovered, the saints and faithful have long known: Prayer works on the fears of the soul and even on the body.

Prayer is more simple and enormously broader than is often allowed by the systems that teach it. It is often made too complicated. I still like my former parishioner's description the best: "We just sit and look at each other." There are many other descriptions: Talking with God, communicating with the Divine, conversing with God, connecting with your higher power, or being open and receptive to God. Mohandas Gandhi said, "Prayer is not asking, it is a longing of the soul." Pope John XXIII considered every aspect of every moment of his life a prayer; no exceptions. Whatever words you use for the Divine in your life, a time spent in that presence heals and lessens fears. The members of Alcoholics Anonymous, as they often do, have come up with a pithy way to say it: Let go; let God. Simply, prayer is an attitude of the heart and an attitude most richly cultivated during the moments, or days, of Stopping.

Aldous Huxley wrote: "We apprehend (God) . . . in the space that separates the salient features of a picture . . . in the pauses and intervals between the notes of music." His statement perfectly ties in prayer with the fundamental idea of Stopping: We find the most important parts of life in the spaces between the notes. God is there, as God is in the spaces of your own life. Huxley adds another, more visually oriented dimension by speaking of the space between the features of a picture as a place to find divine presence. What in art is called negative space—the space between the features—is turned into positive space for those who are Stopping.

Prayer, like Stopping, is the spaces between the notes of life. If you are so inclined, prayer—saying it to God—could be the key way of coping with fears during your Stopping experiences.

We've Had a Hundred Years of Psychotherapy
and the World's Getting Worse

TITLE OF BOOK BY JAMES HILLMAN
AND MICHAEL VENTURA

41

Some Help in Getting Help

Sometimes noticing, naming, narrating, and praying are not enough, and you need help. If you feel you want to get help as you encounter your fears, here are a few ideas about counseling to keep in mind:

First, counseling does not have to go on for a long time. Often, what is now called "brief therapy" (in the range of three to fifteen weeks, once a week) is all that it takes. As much as anything, therapy speeds up the healing, the growth, or the problem-solving processes.

Second, you can get competent help at a reasonable price. You might have to look a little harder, but it is possible. Check out mental health clinics and (non-proselytizing) church-sponsored counseling agencies. Trained pastoral counselors are one of the world's most valuable and best-kept secrets.

Third, maybe more appropriate for you would be a mentor, coach, or spiritual director. A mentor is, generally, an older person who is wise, caring, experienced in what you need to learn, willing to help, and a person you can trust. Normally it is not a paid relationship. A coach, picking up its model from the sports world, is someone who is not a professional therapist, but is someone who cares, has experience and exposure to basic mental health practice, and to whom you can report regularly for encouragement, advice, or direction. It is most often a paid relationship. A spiritual director is a friendly guide and companion who helps you focus specifically on your spiritual life and whose main question is based on "Where and how is God in your life? And what are the implications of that?" This is often a paid relationship, but also sometimes considered part of the service of clergy.

Fourth, most therapy is not for deeply troubled people but for you and me at moments of challenge and opportunity. Most counseling clients just need a little help over the rough spots. So please don't feel embarrassed or ashamed. In the vast majority of cases, therapy is not about a therapist giving advice to an emotionally ill person; it's about any person looking for a safe place and a skilled, wise companion for a particularly challenging part of his or her journey.

Fifth, shop around. If you feel uncomfortable with the therapist you have, for any reason, seek another that you like. The counselor works for you, not the other way around. But, as Hillman and Ventura's intentionally provocative book title at the opening of the chapter implies, all therapy is not equal. Generally, look for counselors that are open to take their starting point from what you report is going on with you, not those who try to squeeze you into a system they happen to practice.

And finally, here's a response to the frequent question: "How do I know when it's time to get into therapy?" Echoing Dr. M. Scott Peck's words, "It's time to get into therapy when you feel you can no longer keep moving ahead by yourself as you deal with your fears; when you're really stuck."

I recall, with some chagrin, going into therapy for the first time. I was studying to be a therapist and it was obligatory in my program to be in therapy. Otherwise, I most likely would not have done it at that time. It took me three months to find a therapist. I know of a professor of psychotherapy who had never been in therapy until a crisis during his retirement (he was sixty-eight) forced him to seek solutions. Talk about resistance!

The therapist I found was a gift. Young, bright, earnest, and Jewish. I wondered at first if this would work: Jewish therapist and priest client. Would he understand my issues? He was skillful. When he did not understand one or another aspect of the Catholic world, he would get me to tell him about it. Thus I was always telling him my stories, which is the best kind of therapy.

I'm afraid if I stop,
I'll never be able to start again!

42

"Yes, but . . . "

Let me anticipate some possible objections to Stopping that might be running through your mind at this point.

Objection: "Look, I already know what will come up for me when I Stop. It's always the same thing, the same old pain (or anger or upset or fear). Why would I want to think of that? It's over and done and there's nothing to be gained but more pain."

Response: The paradox is that the more you move into the same old thing, the less power it will have to cause you pain. The reason it keeps coming up is because it has never been faced or not faced completely. When you keep the door bolted against the big bad wolf, he stays right outside your door, growling, snarling, and constantly reminding you that he's there. Could you be getting used to having him right outside the door? Could it be that in some way you like him there?

I had a wonderful spiritual director in the seminary who was both wise and funny. When I would confess to him, in the pious language of the day, that "I had entertained impure thoughts," he answered, "Heh, heh! Let's get it straight here, kiddo, you didn't entertain them, they entertained you!" So maybe you are used to keeping things out of reach just enough so that they, in some way, "entertain you." Open the door, invite the big bad wolf in, give him a name, get it over with, and move on! (I wonder now what my confessor would have said had I suggested this plan in regard to my "impure" thoughts!)

There's another idea to keep in mind as a response to this objection: creative denial. Sometimes denial is not bad; it can even be beneficial. Healthy denial differs from unhealthy denial because it isn't *really* denial, it's temporary avoidance. You see this clearly in some terminally ill people. "This afternoon I don't have cancer. I don't want anybody to mention it at all," said the twelve-year-old girl to her family on the way from the hospital to an afternoon at the zoo. This is an example of creative denial that was used as a respite from the intensity of a painful reality, and it is healthy. So a healthy-denial-Stopover might not look like a Stopover at all, but it is.

Objection: "I've tried various things like meditation before and, frankly, I get immensely bored. It isn't that I fear anything, it's just that doing nothing bores me so much that I always move on to something that keeps my interest or that is useful."

Response: Start with Stillpoints. They are so short it is impossible to get bored. But at a deeper level, please don't be fooled by boredom. It's often a cover for something else; so begin, like with any feeling, just by noticing it. Stay with it for a while. Then name it; maybe it's a particular kind of boredom: "annoying" or "desperate" or "irksome" or "sleep-inducing." Focus on the boredom rather than letting it focus on you. Move into it. Personify it. "What do you want with me, Boredom? What are you keeping me from?"

Notice that I am making an assumption here: You are not *really* bored. Boring means uninteresting, tiresome, and dull. When you are Stopped, you are alone with yourself, and you are anything but dull. Even though you might see yourself that way, you're not; no one is!

I believe boredom often masquerades as fear of our excellence. Author Marianne Williamson turns fear on its ear when she wonders if just maybe what we are most deeply afraid of "is that we are powerful beyond measure. It is our light, not our darkness, that most frightens us." So perhaps your strongest fear is your wonderfulness. What a concept!

Objection: "As a child of an alcoholic mother, I never knew when it would be safe for me, so I developed an atti-

tude of always watching out for danger. My natural inclination is to pay attention outwardly to other people, not
inwardly to myself. Closing my eyes or paying attention to
myself are things that make me very fearful. I'm always
paying attention to everything around me to keep aware of
what might be coming. I'm afraid Stopping would make
me nervous."

Response: The first response, of course, is to go ahead
and keep your eyes open. Closed eyes are not essential to
Stopping. If it is helpful, you can substitute a trance-like
stare at some point on the floor or wall or at some object;
staring at it but not looking at it or seeing it. I would also
suggest that you concentrate on brief Stillpoints and
include with them a message of self-reassurance, a
reminder that at *this* time and place, you can trust the
security you presume. On a deeper level, in regard to your
discomfort with self-attention, I'd recommend you begin
any longer expressions of Stopping by concentrating on the
gifts of openness and purpose and by examining life in its
most comfortable modes: outside, listening and receptive.
Then, only gradually, move the focus in.

Objection: "I just can't afford it. Yes, it's a great idea in
an ideal world. Who wouldn't love to just do nothing? But
the world is not ideal and there simply are more important
things to do than what you describe as Stopping. No matter how beneficial, by comparison it's frivolous."

Response: Stopping can clearly challenge a person's
very strongly entrenched life pattern of keeping busy,

keeping going, and not looking back. What I would emphasize here are Stillpoints, literally just minutes out of the day and minutes that would normally not be useful for anything else. But, I suspect, it's not just the "frivolous" nature of Stopping that is objectionable, it's the very act of looking at your inner life and is fear masked as seriousness. If you feel something like this, I would suggest that you begin very gradually, just a few Stillpoints a day for a few months. Let yourself slowly get used to the act of looking in. Pick out whatever is helpful in the noticing, naming, and narrating processes; especially in the noticing.

Objection: "I'm afraid that if I stop, really Stop, like in Stopovers or Grinding Halts, I'll never be able to start again. I won't be able to get back into the fast lane, which, because of my work as an emergency room nurse, is where I spend my life. I am afraid that I will be permanently Stopped!"

Response: If you identify with this objection, I would suggest that you treat the statement specifically as a *feeling*, not as a fact. By that I mean, the objection as stated reveals a lot of tiredness and thus its expression is, most likely, primarily an expression of a current feeling rather than a real life fact. Probably you have done an equivalent of a Stopover sometime in your busy life and survived just fine.

By distinguishing between the feeling expressed and the actual fact, you can accept the one as a meaningful expression of what is going on with you at the moment and shine the strong light of reality on the other to test its validity. Start with Stillpoints and remember: You don't have to move on to Stopovers or Grinding Halts unless you want to. For many, Stopping will be primarily expressed in Stillpoints.

Objection: "If I do something, I do it all the way. It's like I have to do all of it or it just won't work. The same with Stopping. My inclination is to immediately do a Grinding Halt of three months. Do the most. Do the best. The rest is not worth it."

Response: This objection, what I call the "All or Nothing," is from a go-for-the-gusto kind of person who brings a lot of energy and enthusiasm to life. I would suggest that the person view Stopping not in a hierarchical, quantitative way, but in a horizontal, qualitative way. Stopping does not go from less good to best; it goes only from this way to that way with no judgment as to which way is better. So a three-month Grinding Halt is not necessarily better for this person than a few Stillpoints spread throughout the day; in fact, it would probably be less effective. The way you choose to do your Stopping depends on your needs, the time available, and all the other variables of the moment. Again, start with Stillpoints.

Objection: "I want to do Stillpoints, I begin every day with the intention of doing them, but I forget. I come to the end of the day without having done even one."

Response: Here's an idea that may help. Find triggers in your day that will call you to a Stillpoint. For example, every time your phone rings, do a Stillpoint before answering it. Every time you get up from your desk (workstation, etc.), do a Stillpoint. Do this every time you go to the bathroom, get a drink of water, use the copy machine, or open a piece of mail. Can you incorporate a reminder for a Stillpoint into your screen saver? As you get in your car, before you start the ignition, or before getting out of your car, take time for a Stillpoint.

The answer to this objection has a lot to do with the idea of intentional living we explored in Chapter 6. Since Stillpoints no longer just happen on their own as they used to, we have to intentionally put them in our lives. Finding things that will serve as triggers will help. Above all, try not to give in to discouragement. It will take awhile to incorporate Stopping into your life. Remember the benefits and stick with it.

I hope that these objections and responses will underline the central place that Stillpoints hold in the process of Stopping. They are the key, the heart and the soul of Stopping. Indeed, many will use only Stillpoints, leaving the Stopovers and Grinding Halts for a later time that might more clearly present itself. But Stillpoints are what will change your life. Gently, by accumulation, these treasured moments will bring you Stopping's gifts. They will also gradually convince you of the desirability and value of Stopovers and Grinding Halts so that you will consider using them in your life as well.

V

Discovering
Your Way
to
Stopping

Normal day, let me be aware of
the treasure you are.
Let me learn from you, love you,
bless you before you depart.

Mary Jean Iron

43

"Stopping by Woods on a Snowy Evening"

What will Stopping look like in your life? What will help you integrate and personalize the three ways of Stopping or help you customize them by discovering your own preferences of how, when, and where Stopping is most likely to happen for you and be most beneficial? This last part of the book will help you to discover how Stopping will fit into your daily, monthly, and yearly routines.

This is where the rubber meets the road. Because if you don't actually Stop, it won't be able to work for you. The choice is yours: to continue to be overwhelmed by your frenetic pace and by the problem of too much; becoming too distracted from what is really important to you—convinced, somehow, that you can't take time out even for a thirty-second Stillpoint—or to begin an easy, simple, and new way of living that will bring you peace, calm, and recollection in the midst of your busy life.

Perhaps saving the best for last, here is a poem that has Stopping in the title: "Stopping by Woods on a Snowy Evening" by Robert Frost. It's a perfect poem for us at this point in the journey. For many it will be familiar. Reading it aloud will emphasize the rhythm and rhyme.

Stopping by Woods on a Snowy Evening
by Robert Frost

Whose woods these are I think I know.
His house is in the village though;
He will not see me stopping here
To watch his woods fill up with snow.

My little horse must think it queer
To stop without a farmhouse near
Between the woods and frozen lake
The darkest evening of the year.

He gives his harness bells a shake
To ask if there is some mistake.
The only other sound's the sweep
Of easy wind and downy flake.

The woods are lovely, dark and deep.
But I have promises to keep,
And miles to go before I sleep,
And miles to go before I sleep.

What a wonderful example of Stopping! He does nothing but stop and watch the woods fill up with snow. That is as close to doing nothing as you get. I have read the poem so often that I have a picture of the narrator in my mind. He is awake and aware of his surroundings, his aloneness in the woods, and the absence of the landowner. And he just sits quietly in the falling snow. He hears the bells, even giving them meaning as his horse's questioning. He feels the woods and names them dark, deep, and lovely.

Then he remembers: I have promises to keep and miles to go before I sleep. That's an important part of who I am, someone with promises to keep and miles to go. And then, we can assume, he returns to his life, wherever he was going when he stopped to watch, now refreshed by his Stopping. (A Christmas errand is hinted at by the "darkest evening" or winter solstice, December 21.)

All the elements of our definition are here: Stopping is doing nothing, to become more fully awake, and remember who you are. Sometimes I take the narrator's place and it is me sitting there in my sleigh . . . watching the snow. Thus reading the poem becomes a Stillpoint.

This poem also reminds us that we are far from the simple life it depicts. For the poet, Stopping was more related to what he was doing in the course of his daily life. His Stopping was at the speed of a sleigh ride; ours is at the speed of light. Either way, Stopping must be chosen.

So we all need to discover our own unique path—the ways, times, places, triggers, occasions, and opportunities— to what I call our "Stopping Woods," for just watching whatever is going on: falling snow or setting sun or growing grass or simply what's outside the window. What will lead you to the brief moments of Stillpoints, to the longer times of Stopovers, and to the occasional extended Stopping of a Grinding Halt?

If you are what you do,
when you don't you aren't.

QUOTED BY WILLIAM J. BYRON, S.J.

44

Permission Granted Just to Be

Based on my Stopping seminars, I've discovered that before traveling the pathway to the Stopping Woods, it is first necessary to give everyone permission to Stop, permission to do nothing, and permission to not feel guilty. Tinged as we are with a rigorous work ethic, a serious attitude about religion, and the general ethos of achievement, it is understandable that we still feel somehow guilty or wrong about doing nothing. In order to incorporate Stopping into our lives, we often need permission. So if you want, and if you will give me the authority, I now grant you permission to do nothing. Here are some voices to back me up:

"We all need to pause before the contemplation of our lives before we can laugh or cry. We are dying for it, literally dying for it," said the poet William Carlos Williams in

1960 shortly before he died. Notice he encourages Stopping—"pause before the contemplation of our lives"—specifically in order to be able to experience the feelings of human life "before we can laugh or cry." When he says "we are dying for it," I believe he means it literally as well as poetically: we are ruining our health because we don't do it.

A more contemporary poet, Maya Angelou, has these words to give you permission: "Each of us needs to withdraw from the cares which will not withdraw from us. We need hours of aimless wandering or spates of time sitting on park benches, observing the mysterious world of ants and the canopy of treetops." I appreciate her image of cares that "will not withdraw from us"—as if they are stuck to us and the only way to be rid of them is with "hours of endless wanderings."

Notice that both poets use the verb *need*. This is not optional. So please take note, we—the poets and I—have now given you permission for Stopping. Will you as willingly and joyfully give it to yourself? That's the real question.

In the Judeo-Christian tradition, God gave the Sabbath as a day to rest. Whatever happened to it? Saturday and Sunday have become as rushed as any Monday. Jesus, who frequently spent time by himself, would also spend forty days and forty nights in the desert, apart and alone. Once he even lectured Martha, who was running around doing things, saying that her sister Mary, who was doing nothing but sitting quietly, had "chosen the better part." He also says, "Come apart and rest awhile." A nun in one of my seminars told how her community augments these words: "Come apart and rest awhile. And if you don't rest awhile, you'll come apart." A good Stopping slogan.

St. Francis was always going off by himself to contemplate, to talk to the animals, to be quiet, and to be alone. Enlightenment came to the Buddha as he was contemplating, sitting quietly under the bodhi tree and doing nothing. Indeed every religious tradition not only gives permission for what I am calling Stopping, but they positively encourage it and speak of it as necessary for any life of grace.

After receiving all this permission, the act of giving *yourself* permission to Stop can lead you to the important developmental discovery of the difference between being a *human doing* and being a *human being*. Giving yourself permission is an act of authority by you and to you. It emphasizes that you are a *you* and not an *it* or an *act*.

William Byron's quote at the start of this chapter points out the danger we all run of being a human doing: if you so identify with what you do—teaching, nursing, repairing, doctoring, cleaning, driving, lawycring, or doing business—then when you are not doing that particular work, you no longer have a sense of who you are; quite literally, you stop being and you lose yourself. On the other hand, if you keep your work as something, albeit a very important something, that you *do*, then you are free to continue *to be* who you have always been and will continue to be no matter what happens in your life.

Medical professors David Waters and Terry Saunders tell of this incident: In frustration a woman asked her husband, a busy physician, "What is it you get at work that you don't get at home?" He thought for a minute and answered, "It's the only time I really feel like I know who I am." Here is a man for whom being and doing are the same thing. This common problem often becomes evident at the moment of changing jobs or professions or at retirement.

Recently in the Pacific Northwest, there were very serious public disputes over logging; environmentalists were on one side and logging-rights activists on the other. In a recent television interview I heard a logger, angry at the possibility of losing his job, say passionately, "I'm a logger. That's what I am!" I believe he was saying, in other words, "If I can't be a logger any more, I don't know what I'll be. And that causes me alarm and panic." The emotional basis for this kind of feeling is the belief: I am what I do.

I can identify with the feelings of both the physician and the logger as I recall my process of leaving the priesthood. Was it something I was or something I did? I am still in the process of getting to the full answer to that question, even though one thing, for me, is sure: neither the logger, nor the physician, nor the priest is essentially that job or role.

So please remember to give yourself permission, maybe quite frequently, to do nothing and to do Stopping. It is a permission that will lead you to *be* who you are and want to become, and, then, to *do* whatever you do.

My soul can find no staircase to heaven
unless it be through earth's loveliness.

MICHELANGELO

45

The Pathway to Your Stopping Woods

To find more answers on how to make Stopping a natural part of your life, come with me through "earth's loveliness" and along the path to the place that will make Stopping easy and enjoyable for you and where you are most likely to actually do it: your Stopping Woods. Along the way, we'll come across many suggestions to help you not only to arrive at your Stopping Woods safely, but be able to visit there whenever you want.

The idea is to pick whatever things that will help you create your own Stopping. I suggest you jot down a list of those things that attract your attention or sound enjoyable to you: those that you know have helped you in the past, those you want to cultivate, and those that you are reminded of as we make our way. These things will help you get to your Stopping Woods. Make your selections thoughtfully and by the end of this short journey, you will probably find that you have all the components—and thus a description—of your personal practice of Stopping.

Reading

What do you read that encourages Stopping or that enhances your meanings and values? All major spiritual traditions have their scriptures or sacred writings: The Torah, the New Testament, the Koran, the Upanishads, the Bhagavad Gita, and others. Would you pick one of these or part of one, such as the Psalms of the Old Testament, the Four Noble Truths of Buddhism, or the Gospel of Mark in the New Testament? Prayer books, containing familiar prayers, psalms, and other sacred texts might be something also to consider. Repetitive reading of favorite texts brings a sense of continuity and familiarity that is important to many.

Small books of daily thoughts or brief aphorisms have become popular in recent years. These are the perfect companions of Stopping. Each day brings a new, provocative, and brief statement that you can use in your Stillpoints throughout the day. You might open a book at random and read what is there as your thought for the day; and each time you do a Stillpoint, you recall your thought.

The Latin term *lectio divina,* literally "divine reading" but most often translated as "spiritual reading," can refer to any reading that deepens your spiritual life, your connection with the divine, or your life of meanings and values. For some, these will be works written specifically for a religious or spiritual purpose, for others, it may also consist of novels or short stories, or it may be anything that brings you closer to God.

As you might guess, poetry is *lectio divina* for me. Reading a brief poem and letting it have its way with me will often be what doing nothing looks like for me during an afternoon Stopover.

What is spiritual reading for you? Don't limit yourself only to the expected sources. Anything goes.

Writing

Does anyone actually write letters anymore? A regular correspondence with a friend can be a wonderful help to Stopping because you have to pause regularly in the process to stop and think about what you want to say and how.

Faxes and e-mail are becoming the contemporary equivalent of letters through the mail. After all, our Stopping is at the speed of light and these means are fast. But remember: just because they are fast, they don't have to be unthoughtful or hurried.

Instead of reading a poem, you can spend a Stopover writing a poem. Why not keep a book of your own poetry?

My brother wrote a forty-page booklet consisting of twenty stories from his life and gave copies to his family. These booklets are a treasure for us and especially for our generations to come. Those stories will tell them something about themselves. I have a niece who has a packet of finished and not-quite finished short stories tucked away in her desk. For many writers of personal stories, the writing is more important than anyone reading them. It reminds us, and we remember.

Journals and diaries are the classic forms of personal writing and are wonderful ways to record the meanings and values of your life; they are the perfect companions, especially for the longer times, of Stopping. The act of writing down the events and feelings of life is to notice them, to give them importance, and to keep them.

Maybe you will just want to collect your own favorite words, phrases, or epigraphs (like the ones at the beginning of the chapters in this book), and keep them in a special place, in a journal, or on your computer.

Visual beauty

"Without beauty there's little fun and less humor," says James Hillman. To that I will add, "without beauty there's impoverished spirituality." For mature human life, beauty, in all its forms, is not optional, and I believe neglect of beauty is one of our most serious and hidden faults. President Kennedy was aware of this when he said one month before he died, "I look forward to an America which will not be afraid of grace and beauty." Beauty needs no intermediary to get to the human soul. It scores a direct hit and stimulates what is best, most noble, and most enjoyable in us. Those creative souls who bring us beauty are our greatest treasures. Too often we benignly ignore them, commercialize them, or, sometimes, stone them.

How can you gather beauty? Don't be limited to just the suggestions here. Are there beautiful pictures in your daily life? Cost is no excuse with all the inexpensive reproductions available. It certainly does not have to be by a famous artist and is better if it's by you. How often do you go to the art museum, a beautiful church, or an architectural gem of a building in your town or city? These (or their equivalents) are not optional niceties, but essential parts of our day for a balanced life, and they are gateways to Stopping. What is beautiful to you? Beauty is in the eye of the beholder. Add it—or a representation of it—to your life.

What colors do you love? Are they all around you? What better way to lift your spirits than to paint your room!

Pin up a photograph or a painting by your computer and let this visual cue lead you to moments—or hours— of Stopping.

Touching

There are so many times we can touch each other. Handshakes, pats on the back, or a gentle hand on the arm; all of these can be a moment of pausing, and, with attention, each can become a Stillpoint. Here's a suggestion: Make every hug a Stillpoint. Breathe, notice where you are, and notice what is important to you.

The textures of cloth on your hand, of food in your mouth, or of anything sensory can signal complexity, simplicity, involvement, or detachment. As you pick up a roughly woven tie or a smooth silk scarf, your Stillpoint message might be: Just like the weave of this tie, there are rough spots in my life right now, but I'll be okay, I'll take care of myself, or May my challenging day turn out to be as smooth as this silk.

Eating meals can be a moment of quiet recognition of our dependence on food and our gratitude for having it. The beginning of a meal is an especially good time to pause for grace. When you eat with others, family or friends, could you call everyone to a moment of prayer, pause, or reflection—a shared Stillpoint? Martin Buber reminds us that when "one eats in holiness . . . the table becomes an altar."

Fast food is what we often eat. Constantly eating fast food is not only contrary to being awake and remembering, it can actually induce spiritual sleep. In Europe, there is an organization called Slow Food: The International Movement for the Defense of and the Right to Pleasure. It was started after McDonalds set up shop in Paris. But fast food is not going away, because it is so cheap and convenient and fits with the other elements of our lives. So when you find yourself grabbing that burger, chugging that soda, or inhaling that pizza, let it serve as a reminder: fast food Stillpoint. Your stomach will thank you and the people you meet the rest of the day will thank you.

And let's remember: eating a meal relatively quickly is not necessarily bad. I believe it is possible to eat a healthy lunch in a healthy way in ten or fifteen minutes if it's done with attention and relaxation. Incessantly eating too fast; not being able to control the speed, timing, and amount of leisure around a meal; and inhaling food with no thoughtfulness of the process—those are bad.

Sexuality can be expressed not only in the moments of lovemaking but in all of the moments of life. You experience it daily as man or as woman, with your particular sensuality and your way of seeing, touching, and appreciating. Erotic energy has accomplished, and will continue to accomplish, wonders for humanity and can lead you to delightful and delicious moments of sexually charged reveries: passionate Stillpoints. From my experience—as a therapist as well as a sexual being—spirituality and sexuality are neighboring facets on the same gem; in the presence of the power of one, the power of the other is always close at hand.

Beautiful sounds and fragrances

I agree with Nietzsche, who said that "life would be a mistake without music" and with Aldous Huxley, who said, "After silence, that which comes nearest to expressing the inexpressible is music." I can't imagine life without it. What about you?

My friend Michael is uncontrollably transported by the sound of certain music. We've been in the middle of a conversation when his eyes roll up in his head, his head tilts back, his arms rise, he begins mouthing the lyrics, and he is somewhere else. An aria from *Madama Butterfly* is playing in the background and Michael is "gone" for a moment. This is an example of the direct hit that beauty makes on the soul and why it is so necessary. It doesn't have to be filtered through the intellect. It is pure, experienced joy.

Vivaldi's *Gloria* is a piece that always scores a direct hit on me. When the combined choruses build to a crescendo of glorious sounds, I'm transported to a pure moment of pleasure: a transcendent Stillpoint.

The sound of a particular voice: Does that lead you to a moment of Stopping? How about the sounds of the ocean, of foghorns, of the wind, of birds, of whales, of trains, or of ships? One of my favorite sounds in the world, and one that will freeze-frame me into a most enjoyable Stillpoint, is the sound of a loon.

Aromatherapy is popular these days but certainly nothing new. Humans and animals have always used scent to attract each other. What are your favorite fragrances? Will burning incense, potpourris, or scented candles lead you to Stopping?

Scents can be powerful reminders of the past, evoking emotions and memories that can lead us to quiet moments of reverie.

Sacramentals

One of the qualities I appreciate about the Catholic tradition is its principle of sacramentality, that is, as theologian Richard McBrien defines it, "the notion that all reality, both animate and inanimate, is potentially or in fact the bearer of God's presence." Thus food, oil, trees, the sun, the moon, the stars, babies' booties, cocker spaniels, and shiny stones—things we can taste, touch, or smell—bring us into contact with the divine. Soulful objects in the valley connect us with transcendent moments on the peaks. Other religious traditions also embody this principle.

Sacramentals are also personal material objects that symbolize something that has great spiritual value or meaning to us. Your grandfather's watch or your mother's ring, perhaps. Anything, really, that symbolizes a value. Think of the things you own and which of them is a sacramental for you. Every time you see it or hold it: a Stillpoint.

Talismans and charms are types of sacramentals and are often designed with the intention of being held in your hand to remind you of what they symbolize. In my workshops, I give participants a small, green, plastic stop sign to carry in their pocket as a reminder and to hold as needed for a Stillpoint. The shape is a reminder to Stop; the color is a reminder that Stopping is ultimately for going.

Rituals

Therapists Janine Roberts and Evan Imber-Black in *Rituals for Our Times* describe rituals as bestowing "protected time and space to stop and reflect on life's transformations" and as offering "opportunities to make meaning from the familiar and the mysterious at the same time." There are the common family rituals of birthday cakes, wedding celebrations, bedtime stories, and good-night kisses, and religious rituals like baptism, bar mitzvah, the mass, the seder, and the many forms of prayer such as novenas, devotions, and making the sign of the cross. If you take just a moment, I'm sure you can think of rituals that are unique to your family. All of these can be expressions of Stopping because they bring you to a moment or moments of quiet and they are reminders of who you are that can awaken you to the present.

But what about bringing ritual to the more common moments of life? What about creating your personal rituals around the events that carry meaning for you? Do you have rituals around exercise or eating or sleeping or vacations or Sunday mornings or, perhaps, the day you made a life-changing decision? Note the occasion with a simple remembering ritual, perhaps a recollection, a prayer, a brief visit to a place, or the lighting of a candle. At dinner, remind your family or meal companion(s) what anniversary this is—the day Grandfather died, the day your child was baptized, or a day important to the ethnicity of your family—and invite them to a moment of quiet reflection on the event so that everyone enjoys a Stillpoint together.

At those times when you are eating alone, it is especially rewarding to recall some meaningful event or person and ritualize it by unobtrusively toasting with your cup of tea or inviting them to join you in spirit for this meal.

Spaces and places

At a particular point on the trail I often follow in the park near my home, there is one place where I can see Mount Tamalpais to the west and Mount Diablo to the east. It is a sacred place for me. I pause every time I pass the spot, and I take time for a Stillpoint.

Mountains? Deserts? Which calls to you? Where are you most at home and most yourself? To which of the natural places do you head when you want comfort, consolation, and acceptance?

I feel fortunate to live on the northern California coast, a blessed place if ever there was one. The Pacific Ocean is astounding, no matter the time of day or year; it calls to the deep in us. Lakes, rivers, and for many, like Henry David Thoreau, even ponds can be sacred places of quiet and meaning. "I went to [Walden Pond] because I wished to live deliberately . . ." Do you have a Walden Pond? A Walden River? A Walden Lake?

For many people, sacred spaces are of human origin: museums or churches, for example. For me the rotunda at the National Gallery of Art in Washington, D.C., is such a place. When I go there I feel transported to another level, and experience a feeling of calm and appreciation. Why? I don't know. Who is not struck dumb on entering the cathedral in Florence? Or even, perhaps, a small church in your neighborhood?

Animals

What joy animals can bring to our lives! One only has to watch a boy with his dog, a grandmother with her cat, or perhaps you with your pet to know the power of animal connection. We know that holding an animal can physio-logically bring calm and a sense of well-being. If you have a pet, touching or petting or otherwise connecting with it can be the most consistent and rewarding way of integrat-ing Stillpoints into your daily life. Make it your intention that every time you connect with your pet, you will take a breath, be aware of the moment, and bring to mind what you need to remember.

Animals can also serve as symbols of particular virtues or qualities that we want to incorporate into our lives: the courage of a lion, the loyalty of a dog, or the playfulness of a cat. Thus the sight of the animal or its representation can call us to a Stillpoint and remember the quality we emulate.

You can see an animal as a totem, as an emblem of your own self, or as a guardian spirit. For years my niece and I have been wilderness traveling-companions, needing no excuse to get a group together and strike out in canoes or kayaks. During those excursions we have come to know our totems as the bear (mine) and the dolphin (hers). They have become meaningful symbols, emblems of what we need or appreciate in our lives and of what we want to achieve.

Seasons, weather, and movements of the earth

Winter, spring, summer, fall, rain, sun, wind, fog, snow, hail, mist, holy days, liturgical seasons, holiday seasons, or family birthdays: all of these and many more can be occasions for Stillpoints and sometimes for Stopovers as well. All of these seasons and conditions are pregnant with meaning—coziness of winter, new life of spring, playfulness of summer, and the advancing darkness of autumn.

Every day of every year offers many occasions for Stillpoints merely by noticing that we are outside or by noticing the calendar or season and letting them lead you to what you need in the moment.

As I am writing this, our planet has just been visited by the comet Hale-Bopp. It has been the occasion of wonderful Stillpoints for me. It started on my birthday while I was having dinner with family and friends in the Napa Valley. It was a beautifully clear and crisp night in spring. We were seated in the restaurant's outdoor portico with a fire crackling in the fireplace nearby. To the east, I looked up to watch an eclipse of the moon; to the west, I looked up to watch Hale-Bopp soaring through space. The combination of visible cosmic drama, significant birthday, perfect company, and the beauty of the place provided me not only with several Stillpoints that evening, but with many more, even to this moment, in the remembering.

This listing—this journey down the pathway to your Stopping Woods—is just a hint of what can call you to a time of Stopping. Be sure to spend a moment gathering your thoughts or making a list of the kinds of things that especially call you. They might not be the expected things like holy objects or seasons of the year; they may even seem quite odd.

One of mine is fishponds. When I was very young— maybe four or five, Petey, a little boy down the street who was younger than I, drowned in the fishpond in his back-yard. It was my first encounter with death, and it happened in a place with which I was familiar and where I had often played. It had a profound effect on me. From that day to this, I don't see or hear of a fishpond without thinking briefly of Petey and the fragility of life and the need to make every moment count: a Stillpoint.

Does anything come to your mind that might be unusual triggers for your Stopping? Perhaps you can keep your list handy and continue your process of defining how you will incorporate Stopping into your daily routine.

You can't get there from here.

46

Stopping while Going from Here to There

Especially when you are thinking that poet Ogden Nash's words make perfect sense and Stopping feels like something that you can't get to from where you are now, it is important to remember this: Stopping often takes place most easily during a time of transition from one event to another or from one place to another, whether it is a Stillpoint between appointments, on the way to or from work, on a Stopover weekend between work weeks, or on a Grinding Halt between life stages, it is a powerful "pause between the notes." To identify your most common transition is a significant step toward incorporating Stopping into your life.

241

I suppose the most typical transition time for most people is the daily commute. For commuters, Stillpoints can transform this time from horror to haven. If you were to see these moments (or for some, hours) of transition as welcome pauses or rests wherein you can Stop, you might even look forward to them.

If you drive your car to work, you are probably thinking, as I have often thought, "in that horrible traffic, as tired and hot as I often feel, as frustrating as my day has been, how could I possibly look forward to that time?" But it is possible to incorporate Stillpoints into your drive. And believe me: you'll feel better.

Obviously, the only parts of the Stillpoint that won't work while driving are the optional parts of closing your eyes and diverting your attention or anything which would endanger you on the road. Your first concern must be to remain alert and attentive to the act of driving. But there is still much you can do within those parameters. The driving Stillpoint will be less introspective, and will be more geared to your physical and mental comfort.

Recall the idea from part I about intentional living: the need to take the things of daily life out of the realm of habitual routine and into the realm of conscious choice. It applies here: You can intentionally turn drive time into Stopping time. Choose to consciously breathe every time you reach a red light or stop sign or every time someone cuts you off. Choose music that soothes, choose the Stillpoint message you need to hear, choose to put this time in the hands of God, choose to use positive vocabulary when talking and thinking of commuting, and, lastly, choose to see your commute time not as horrible and something you have to endure, but as valuable and something that enhances your life, your powerful pause, and your rest between the notes. From now on: Drive time is Stillpoint time.

Trains, buses, airplanes, and boats all are ideal places for Stillpoints. They have the advantage of leaving the driving to someone else so that your Stillpoints can be more complete and effective.

What are some other transition times in your life? Every day is filled with them: from asleep to awake, from bathroom to bedroom, from breakfast to the car, from school to work, and from weekday to weekend. In other words, transition time is *from* any one thing or place or time *to* any other thing or place or time; they are all the "from-to's" of your life.

So whenever it feels like you can't get from here (wherever you are) to there (Stopping), think of transitions. What are you in-between? Where are you coming from? Where are you going? What was last and what is next? As the nature and needs of your transitions are identified, the specific way of Stopping will also become clear.

All walking is discovery.
On foot we take the time
to see things whole.

HAL BORLAND

47

Moving while Stopping

There are some people who just have a very difficult time keeping still, that is, maintaining their body in a non-moving mode for any length of time. This immediately makes me think of Carla. When I am with her, I am constantly aware that she never stops jiggling her legs, moving here, going there, or gesticulating unendingly. She has a very hard time staying still. There's nothing at all wrong with that; it's just her nature. Whenever I feel anxious, I can identify with Carla: I don't want to sit still, it bothers me, and I need to move.

Henry David Thoreau understands Carla, too. In his essay "Walking," he says, "I think that I cannot preserve my health and spirits, unless I spend four hours a day at least—and it is commonly more than that—sauntering

245

through the woods and over the fields." For these folks, as well as for all of us, Stopping can be done while moving.

In his essay, Thoreau chose the word *sauntering*. In the same essay he speaks of sauntering as a word which "is beautifully derived 'from idle people who roved about the country, in the Middle Ages, and asked charity, under pretense of going *'á la Sainte Terre,'* to the Holy Land, till the children exclaimed, 'There goes a Sainte-Terrer,' (thus saunterer) a Holy-Lander. . . . They who never go to the Holy Land in their walks . . . are indeed mere idlers and vagabonds." So, walking is made for the holy land of Stopping.

How about jogging-Stopping? This would seem more challenging, at least for me, but maybe not for you. I think it would be difficult to maintain a quality of calm and attentiveness while moving quickly. Thoreau slows walking down to sauntering; running or jogging speeds it up. Recalling the equation of "Speed is to forgetting as slowness is to remembering" would seem to bear this out. Working out in a gym or at home would seem to fall into the same speed category. There is a lot of physical exertion and concentration involved. I think these high-energy activities could start with, pause in the middle for, and end with Stillpoints, and thus transform the entire exercise experience into something beyond physical development. But this surely is a matter of individual preference.

During a recent workshop, I asked how people had experienced Stopping in their lives. Immediately Bill spoke up and said, "On the golf course." He explained his inward state of mind; his peacefulness; and how, by focusing on hitting the ball, he is free to let everything else go. "I often have to be reminded that it's my turn to play."

There is another important way to move and Stop at the same time: pacing. I discovered pacing when I was a seminary student, and I have used it regularly since then. Pacing is slowly walking a predetermined and repetitive course while mentally concentrating on something else. Walking in circles while praying the rosary is how I discovered its value. In the seminary, every day at five o'clock the afternoon bell would sound; all talking would immediately cease and the seminarians would take out their rosaries, cast their eyes down, and begin to walk around the grounds, silently pacing. The Buddhists call this walking meditation.

You might like to try pacing. I find it especially helpful when I am feeling anxious or nervous for any reason. Pick out a safe course, inside or outside. The course must be predictable, safe, and repeatable. Pace back and forth in your room or office, in a circle in the yard, in a park, or anywhere; you don't need a lot of room for this. Rather than close your eyes, you can cast them down at the ground. The moving seems to soothe the anxiety and because your course is safe and predictable—you don't have to pay attention to where you are physically going— you can in fact be still in your soul: a Stillpoint.

The ultimate in pacing is the labyrinth. The labyrinth is an ancient, universal image of life, a large circle with a clear, winding path from the outside to the center and back. (Not to be confused with a maze, which has blind ends and tricks). The California Pacific Medical Center, which has a labyrinth in its courtyard for its patients and staff, calls it "a sacred path to health and wholeness." People are encouraged to walk, run, or dance—most walk slowly—in and out of the sacred circle.

Dr. Lauren Artress of San Francisco's Grace Cathedral is mainly responsible for bringing the ancient practice to contemporary awareness. In her book, *Walking a Sacred Path: Rediscovering the Labyrinth as a Spiritual Tool,* she describes the labyrinth as offering "a sacred and stable place to focus the attention and listen to the longing of the soul" and as a "tool to guide healing, deepen self-knowledge and empower creativity."

Walking the labyrinth is the epitome of moving while Stopping. Dr. Artress says that for many who have walked the labyrinth—and I am surely one of them—"time seems to stand still." Yes! There! That's it!

To live is so startling
it leaves little time
for anything else.

48

The Young, the Old,
and the Violent

I hope you've gotten the idea that Stopping is a very adaptable process. People will tend to develop their own style, and any given person might well do Stopping in different ways at different times. There are very few rules and no dogmas at all; that is, Stopping has no content in the form of beliefs or doctrines. It is pure process and can fit with any spiritual system and with any person's style. The idea is simply to achieve enough quiet and enough stillness to hear the truth, both within and without.

Some folks will prefer to keep moving during their Stillpoints, while others will prefer to stay quite physically still. Some will be on a golf course and some will be in a chapel.

x

249

For Stopovers, some will stay home and others will go far away. Some will be attracted to the long times of Grinding Halts and do them several times in their lives, while others will never do one. Some will . . . well, you get the idea. Please keep in mind however, that the great thing about the Stillpoints expression of Stopping is that *you can do them in any way, in any place, and all the time.*

There are three groups of people for whom Stopping offers special implications and challenges. They are the young, the old, and the violent.

Children and adolescents

The general assumption in the book is that we are speaking to and about adults. And in general, adults are the ones who most need Stopping and have most of the power (money and influence) to make it happen. But both adolescents and children need Stopping as much as we do and, in some ways, they can teach us a lot about it.

If you have any experience with adolescents, you know that they can be very spacey or distracted from what you think they should be attending to. Although frustrating, it's a normal and important part of their development and, in a manner of speaking, it is one of their ways of Stopping, of taking time out from all the challenges of life, and of trying to remember who they are and what's important to them. Because we associate it with the awkward and frustrating years of adolescence, we miss the value of doing our own variety of spacing out; it might feel too juvenile.

And, of course, the Stopping ability of young children is legendary. One need only watch a lone child at play to notice and learn.

We need to take lessons from the younger members of our families. Really though, it is not a lesson we need to learn as much as it is a memory we need to recapture, for we too were their age and had their same native expertise. We just lost it.

More than anything, we adults can help by creating times, places, and opportunities for Stopping for the young people in our lives. Help them notice the pauses between their notes and the value of them. Of course the first comment your efforts might bring is, "Mom, I'm bored!" or "Dad, there's nothing to do!" but with persistence and example on our part, they may learn the value of Stopping.

The elderly

The real pros at Stopping are old people. In the dedication of this book, I indicate that my father was an example to me of how to use Stopping. This was most especially true in his later years. He enjoyed over twenty years of retirement and was very content doing very little and spending many hours simply Stopped. As he went through his losses—ability to play golf, sufficient eyesight for reading, and adequate hearing for normal conversation—he just remained quiet, contemplating and remembering.

My father was not one to tell you his feelings at any great length, but when he did, it was often worth noting. My mother tells this story: One evening, just a few years before Dad's death at ninety-one, my parents were sitting in their chairs, as they did every evening. Probably my mother was reading and Dad was just sitting quietly. Out of the blue he said to her, "You know, dear, I think I need a computer." My mother literally dropped her book in amazement and exclaimed, "A computer? What on earth for?" My father's response: "To count my blessings."

The challenge is to get smart before we get too old—too old to learn or even to change. By developing Stopping now, our years of old age and loss are much more likely to be sweet and calm; you won't be a dear old man or woman unless you are continually becoming a dear younger one. Old Scrooge, in Dickens' *A Christmas Carol,* really had it easy. Only three terrifying visitors in one miserable night and he became a new man. For the rest of us, it's night by night and day by day.

The violent

I have no idea what to do about the incredible violence that we visit upon ourselves. I watch in amazement and horror the TV ads for movies and television programs filled with terrible human violence, and I read the many news items of murder and mayhem among the young. I know that I am not the only one who feels this way; most of the people I speak with feel the same. It must be because people in power believe that money is always the bottom line and this stuff sells. But why does it sell? I still have no real answer . . . except Stopping. It is at least a start.

At first it feels, even to me, a very naive answer. But when I think it through, I come to a point of conviction: The only thing that will change the pattern and habit of violence in people is the only thing that has ever morally transformed people—conversion; a turning around of the way one sees things. In order to do that, we must help people Stop, because Stopping is a necessary condition for a change of heart. You can't change if you are not still enough, long enough, to see that there is a different way or better way. Violent people—that's all of us, potentially— are so hugely and profoundly distracted that the better way is literally unimaginable.

Let the youth on the street Stop. Let the network CEOs Stop. Let the actors who portray such horrors Stop. Let the newspaper editors Stop. Let the parents Stop. Let the teachers Stop. Let the men Stop. Let the women Stop. Let the children Stop. Let me and you Stop.

Caring is the greatest thing,
caring matters most.

FRIEDRICH VON HUGEL

49

Stopping Is Caring

I believe at this point it is clear that Stopping aims to access those most personal issues, feelings, and truths that are in the heart and soul of each of us and that help us to realize our purpose, and to help us know who we are and what and who is important to us. But Stopping, especially if you stick with it for a while, goes beyond those questions to the bigger, broader ones that affect the world. In fact, in looking at our most personal issues and desires, we can thereby naturally be led out of ourselves to the needs of the world's communities.

It is a natural outcome of Stopping to gain a heightened awareness of one's surroundings, both close in and far away. It is an inevitable result; one just begins to notice

255

more and more. This leads, by a natural progression, to an examination of the relationship between Stopping and environmental awareness, both locally and globally. Thus, the most passionate heart of Stopping is a deep forest-green.

Naturalist Bill McKibben understands Stopping. I know this from reading his introduction and annotations to a fine, new edition of Thoreau's *Walden*. He describes a one-week backpack trip, beginning with the challenge of the noise of internal chatter, through the time when the "chatter in [his] head began to subside," and to the point, at nightfall, when he was watching a blue heron and "the sky blackened, the stars spread across the sky bright and insistent; we were unimaginably small, this heron and I, and extremely *right.*" These are the words of someone who notices and especially of someone who cares. Stopping leads to caring.

And caring invariably leads to questions. From McKibben's reading of *Walden*, Thoreau, whom he wonderfully describes—capturing his peculiarly American spirit—as a "Buddha with a receipt from the hardware store," poses two essential questions for our times. The first question stands as an "assault on the Information Age," on computers and all the fast systems of communicating: "How can I hear my own heart?" The second, which I believe flows from the first, is addressed to all of us who make up the consumer society: "How much is enough?" Is constant growth the best for us all? The illness of the Age of Anxiety—cancer—offers us a valuable and provocative symbol for our times: cancer is uncontrolled growth.

These two questions, "How can I hear my own heart?" and "How much is enough?" are wonderful examples of the kinds of questions that we can look at, understand, get a feel for, develop a sense of, and, especially, care about and maybe even begin to answer through our on-going practice of Stopping.

The only thing that keeps us from floating
off with the wind is our stories.
They give us a name and put us in a place,
allow us to keep on touching.

Tom Spanbauer,
The Man Who Fell in Love with the Moon

50

Trust Yourself

More than anything, I hope that Stopping will help
you gather into your consciousness all the wonderful
stories of your life—and they're *all* wonderful. These are
what will lead you to your truths and, thus, to what is
best for the world. Stories are a "connection to our roots,
to where we come from. Through stories we can understand our lives," says Joe Bruchac, storyteller and writer.
Storytelling is "almost like calling the gods. A powerful
spiritual presence makes itself felt, and one can be quite
literally swept away by it."

But we often miss the stories that are ours and that come
to us from our ancestors, because, adds storyteller Laura
Simms, "modern life, with all its noise and distractions,

makes these stories difficult to hear." Stopping prepares us
to hear them.

Bruno Bettleheim, child psychologist and educator, saw
fairy tales as medicine for the soul. The fairy tale is thera-
peutic "because the patient finds his *own* solutions, through
contemplating what the story seems to imply about him
and his inner conflicts." Clarissa Pinkola Estés also sees the
healing power of stories. In a recent radio interview she too
compared stories to medicine: "the flow of images in stories
is [a] medicine [that] acts like an antibiotic that finds the
source of the infection and concentrates there. The story
helps make that part of the psyche clear and strong again."

Is your child out of sorts? Perhaps you can find her or
his medicine in a storybook. Try to pick one out that will
speak to her or his heart. And you? When are you out of
sorts? What story do you need to remind you? A Stillpoint
might bring you just the right one, perhaps one you had
not remembered for a long time, from a book or from your
life or one you had not thought of as a story.

One way to look at all of life is to see it as one story
after another and as stories that we are telling both to ourselves and to everyone else. For example, try The Story
of Yesterday—your yesterday. Begin it with something
like, "I awoke way too early, I think it was about 5 A.M.,
and began to think about my project. . . ." continue
through, "Then just after a quick lunch I ran into Harvey
whom I hadn't seen in months. We spent ten minutes
catching up and decided . . . " and end, perhaps, with,

"I finally flopped into bed at eleven and dreamed that I was. . . . "

I hope Stopping can help you discover the stories of your life. There's something about pausing that invites the remembering of stories, and there is something about stories that just wants to be told. One way of expressing friendship is to tell each other your stories as well as live some of them together. Isn't that what a family does? And family can include anyone you want it to. Ask your parents and grandparents for their stories. Tell your children yours. Share them with your friends. After all, asks Shed in Tom Spanbauer's novel, *The Man Who Fell in Love with the Moon*, "what's a human being without a story?"

Another of my hopes is that Stopping will bolster your trust in yourself so that when you are confronted with the question, "Is the story I'm telling crazy, or is it the rest of the world?" you will answer, "It's the rest of the world!" Carl Jung acknowledged it years ago. Craziness today has been institutionalized. Our citizens, individually, are mostly sane and reasonable; it's our institutions that are nuts! And we take on that craziness because we have to work within the framework of these institutions. The popularity of the comic strip "Dilbert" is a perfect example of our recognition of this, it points out the absurdity of his company's rules and procedures as well as their continued existence. Let's hope corporate craziness is a phase and is, perhaps, a necessary step in reaching for flexible systems that put people first. Developing the habit of Stopping will help continue to convince you of your sanity.

This idea has a corollary for people with the responsibility of children. With all the talk of dysfunctional families going on these days, I hope that Stopping leads us to recognize all systems to one degree or another are dysfunctional. *And* that many families are *quite functional* and send their children out into very dysfunctional—that is crazy—social systems and worldly institutions. A family, no matter how it is configured, that Stops, is a family more prepared to face that contemporary reality and still thrive.

Lastly, I hope that it is clear by now: Stopping is fundamentally optimistic and hopeful. The process of Stopping is based on the belief that you are perfectly fine just the way you are and that you will continue to discover more and more of your own truth, beauty, and goodness if you just make time for Stopping.

Bibliography

Artress, Lauren. *Walking a Sacred Path: Rediscovering the Labyrinth as a Spiritual Tool.* New York: Riverhead Books, 1995.

Becker, Ernest. *The Denial of Death.* New York: The Free Press, 1973.

Benson, Herbert. *Beyond the Relaxation Response.* New York: Berkeley Books, 1985.

Bly, Robert. *A Little Book on the Human Shadow.* Edited by William Booth. San Francisco, CA: Harper and Row, 1988.

Boorstein, Sylvia. *Don't Just Do Something, Sit There: A Mindfulness Retreat.* San Francisco, CA: HarperSanFrancisco, 1996.

Buechner, Frederick. *Listening to Your Life: Daily Meditations with Frederick Buechner.* Compiled by George Connor. San Francisco, CA: HarperSanFrancisco, 1992.

Cooper, David. *Silence, Simplicity, and Solitude.* New York: Bell Tower, 1992.

Covey, Stephen. *The Seven Habits of Highly Effective People: Restoring the Character Ethic.* New York: Simon and Schuster, 1989.

Dowrick, Stephanie. *Intimacy and Solitude.* New York: W. W. Norton, 1991.

Fields, Rick, et al. *Chop Wood Carry Water: A Guide to Finding Spiritual Fulfillment in Everyday Life.* Los Angeles, CA: Jeremy P. Tarcher, Inc., 1984.

Frost, Robert. *The Poetry of Robert Frost*. New York: Holt, Rinehart and Winston, 1969.

Griffin, David Ray, ed. *Spirituality and Society*. New York: State University of NY, 1988.

Groves, Dawn. *Meditation for Busy People*. Novato, CA: New World Library, 1993.

Grumbach, Doris. *Fifty Days of Solitude*. Boston: Beacon Press, 1994.

Halpern, Sue. *Migrations to Solitude*. New York: Random House, 1992.

Hanh, Thich Nhat. *The Miracle of Mindfulness*. Boston: Beacon Press, 1976.

Hanson, Peter. *The Joy of Stress*. New York: Andrews, McMeel and Parker, 1985.

Harp, David. *The Three Minute Mediator*. Oakland, CA: New Harbinger, 1996.

Hillman, James. *The Soul's Code*. New York: Random House, 1996.

_____. *A Blue Fire*. Selected writings introduced and edited by Thomas Moore. New York: HarperCollins, 1989.

_____, & Michael Ventura. *We've Had a Hundred Years of Psychotherapy and the World's Getting Worse*. San Francisco, CA: HarperSanFrancisco, 1992.

Huber, Cheri. *There Is Nothing Wrong with You*. Mountain View, CA: Keep It Simple Books, 1993.

Imber-Black, E., & J. Roberts. *Rituals for Our Times*. New York: HarperCollins, 1992.

Jung, Carl G. *Memories, Dreams, Reflections*. New York: Random House, 1961.

Kabat-Zinn, Jon. *Wherever You Go There You Are*. New York: Hyperion, 1994.

_____. *Full Catastrophe Living*. New York: Delta, 1990.

_____. *Everyday Blessings: The Inner Work of Mindful Parenting*. New York: Hyperion, 1997.

Katherine, Anne. *Boundaries: Where You End and I Begin.* New York: Simon and Schuster, 1991.

Kelly, Jack, & Marcia Kelly. *Sanctuaries: The Complete United States.* New York: Bell Tower, 1996.

Kornfield, Jack. *A Path with Heart.* New York: Bantam Books, 1993.

Kundera, Milan. *Slowness.* New York: HarperCollins, 1995.

Kurtz, E., &, K. Ketcham. *The Spirituality of Imperfection.* New York: Bantam Books, 1992.

Levine, Stephen. *Who Dies?* Garden City, N.Y.: Anchor Books, 1982.

Machado, Antonio. *Times Alone: Selected Poems of Antonio Machado Chosen and Translated by Robert Bly.* Wesleyan University Press, 1983.

Miller, Emmett. *Professional Manual and Desk Reference.* Menlo Park, CA: Source Cassettes, 1980. (Also: audio cassettes on stress Management, relaxation, and other topics.)

Moore, Thomas. *Care of the Soul.* New York: HarperCollins, 1992.

_____. *The Re-Enchantment of Everyday Life.* New York: Harper-Collins, 1996.

Neruda, Pablo. *Extravagaria.* Translated by Alastair Reid. Austin, TX: University of Texas Press, 1969.

Ornstein, R. & D. Sobel. *Healthy Pleasures.* Reading, MA.: Addison-Wesley, 1989.

Peck, M. Scott. *The Road Less Traveled and Beyond: Spiritual Growth in an Age of Anxiety.* New York: Simon and Schuster, 1997.

Rechtschaffen, Stephan. *Timeshifting. Creating More Time to Enjoy Your Life.* New York: Doubleday, 1996.

Rilke, Rainer Maria. *Selected Poems of Rainer Maria Rilke.* Translation and Commentary by Robert Bly. New York: Harper and Row, 1981.

Siegel, Bernie S. *Love, Medicine, and Miracles.* New York: Harper and Row, 1988.

Storr, Anthony. *Solitude.* New York: The Free Press, 1988.

Thoreau, Henry David. *Walden.* Introduction and Annotation by Bill McKibben. Boston: Beacon Press, 1997.

_____. *Walking: An Abridgement of the Essay.* Berkeley, CA: The Nature Company, 1993.

Whitfield, Charles. *Boundaries and Relationships.* Deerfield Beach, Fla.: Health Communications, 1993.

Wilson, Paul. *Instant Calm: Over 100 Easy-to-Use Techniques for Relaxing Mind and Body.* New York: Plume (Penguin), 1995.

Yalom, Irving. *Love's Executioner and Other Tales of Psychotherapy.* New York: HarperCollins, 1989.

Zweig, C. & J. Abrams, eds. *Meeting the Shadow: The Hidden Power of the Dark Side of Human Nature.* New York: G. P. Putnam's Sons, 1991.

Acknowledgments

I want to express my sincere thanks and appreciation:

To Mary Elyn Bahlert, for the many enjoyable hours of discussion and encouragement at the Imperial Cafe. To Jeff Kunkel, who liked my ideas and who was the right person with the right skills to help me find the right voice. To Tom West, who read the manuscript and offered valuable suggestions and support. To Joe, Michael, and Tom, my three companions in our reading group who, in addition to talking books, shared life. Thanks, you guys. To Chilton Thomson, an extraordinary teacher, who many years ago was the first to call forth from my soul a desire for reading and writing. And to Robert Stenberg, in whom I first recognized and appreciated the use and value of Stillpoints.

Also thanks to my agent, Carol Susan Roth, who helped in the development of the book, who guided me with good humor to the right publisher, and who lives up to her description as "an author's best friend." To Kevin Davis, whose NSA workshop was a quantum leap in my learning process.

And to Mary Jane Ryan—I met her last year but I've known her all my life—of Conari Press. I could not wish for a more skilled, insightful, and caring editor. And to all the great folks at Conari Press, thanks.

Permissions Acknowledgments

About the Author

David J. Kundtz, author, speaker and counselor, is a psychotherapist in private practice and director of the Berkeley, California–based Inside Track Seminars, which offers workshops in the areas of human resources, stress management, and emotional health. Ordained in 1963, he was a priest for nineteen years, serving in the Catholic Diocese of Boise, Idaho, and in Cali, Colombia, South America.

He has earned graduate degrees in both psychology and theology and his doctoral degree, a doctor of science and theology (S.T.D.), is in the field of pastoral psychology. He is a member of the National Speakers Association, the California Association of Marriage and Family Therapists, the American

Seminar Leaders Association and the American Counseling Association. His prvious book was *Men and Feelings*. He lives in Kensington, California, and Vancouver, British Columbia.

Dr. Kundtz warmly welcomes your communication, especially your experiences, insights, challenges and successes with Stopping.

Send e-mail to: dk@stopping.com
fax: (510) 559-9193
Write: David Kundtz, c/o Conari Press,
2550 Ninth Street, Suite 101,
Berkeley, California 94710-2551

Visit the Stopping web site at: www.stopping.com